Mastering Social Work Supervision

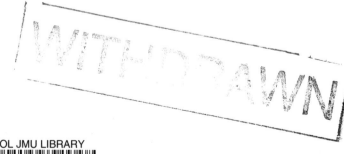

Mastering Social Work Skills series

Edited by Jane Wonnacott

This series of short, accessible books focuses on the everyday key skills that social workers need in order to practise effectively and ensure the best possible outcomes for service users. Easy to read and practical, the books feature key learning points, practice examples based on real-life situations, and exercises for the reader to enhance their learning. The books in this series are essential reading for post-qualifying social work students and social work practitioners.

Jane Wonnacott is Director of In-Trac Training and Consultancy, UK.

other books in the series

Mastering Approaches to Diversity in Social Work
Linda Gast and Anne Patmore
ISBN 978 1 84905 224 5

MASTERING
Social Work
Supervision

Jane Wonnacott

Jessica Kingsley *Publishers*
London and Philadelphia

Figure 4.7 'The Decision Tree' reproduced by permission of SAGE Publications, London, Los Angeles, New Delhi and Singapore, from *Effective Child Protection* (2008) 2nd Edition, by Eileen Munro.

First published in 2012
by Jessica Kingsley Publishers
116 Pentonville Road
London N1 9JB, UK
and
400 Market Street, Suite 400
Philadelphia, PA 19106, USA

www.jkp.com

Library of Congress Cataloging in Publication Data
A CIP catalog record for this book is available from the Library of Congress

British Library Cataloguing in Publication Data
A CIP catalogue record for this book is available from the British Library

ISBN 978 1 84905 177 4
eISBN 978 0 85700 403 1

Printed and bound in Great Britain

CONTENTS

Figures and Tables

Series Editor Foreword

When social workers have confidence in their own skills, purpose and identity, and in the system in place to back them up, they have a huge amount to offer. They collaborate effectively with other professionals and adapt to new roles and expectations. Most importantly, they forge constructive partnerships with people who find themselves vulnerable or at risk and make a sustained difference in their lives.

Report of the Social Work Task Force (2009, p.5)

This book forms part of a series which aims to increase social work confidence by exploring the essential skills that social workers need to do their job and giving accessible, practical ideas based on evidence from research and practice.

The series challenges the view that social work is about 'doing the simple things well', a view that has taken hold in some circles since publication of the Laming report in 2003. Social work is not simple; it is a complex activity, and social workers are working with risk and uncertainty on a day-to-day basis.

It is the premise of this series that good social work involves the capacity to develop and maintain relationships, manage the emotional dimension of the work and make judgements and decisions, often in the light of conflicting information. This is demanding work and will only be effective if social workers are encouraged to reflect critically on their practice and to continue developing their knowledge and skills. Too often the time for reflection and skill development is minimal, and social workers rely on prescriptive procedures that do not always assist the creativity and critical thinking that are fundamental to good, safe practice.

The starting point for authors of this series is a positive expectations model, that is, one based on the assumption that social workers want to do a good job and need flexible tools and frameworks to help them practise in the challenging environment within which they work. The authors are experienced social work trainers and practitioners and the content of each book is based on material that has been extensively tested with front-line practitioners and their managers.

A comment on the title

The series has been entitled 'Mastering Social Work' because it aims to move beyond basic skills to those which may support the practitioner in more challenging circumstances. 'Mastering' is a process of developing expertise by applying learning and knowledge to practice. It is a continuous activity. Our aim and hope is that this series will assist social workers in this task by providing ideas and frameworks to support them in their day-to-day work.

'Mastering' is a gendered term. We have thought carefully about its use in a social work context and have searched for alternatives but there are no others that convey its intended meaning here – a process of developing exceptional skill.

PREFACE

> It is vitally important that social work is carried out in a supportive learning environment that actively encourages the continuous development of professional judgement and skills. Regular, high quality, organised supervision is critical.
>
> Lord Laming (2009)

If social workers are to develop expertise and mastery of their profession, the role of the supervisor is crucial. The quality of individual supervisory relationships can have a profound influence on, not only the social worker themselves, but outcomes for users of social work services. Although complex and challenging both emotionally and intellectually social work should be endlessly fascinating and rewarding. It is though supervision that social workers can be supported developed and encouraged to think differently and creatively whilst always maintaining a focus on the best interests of service users. This book is therefore based on a belief that good supervision is the cornerstone of good, safe, creative social work practice and that support and training for supervisors is one of the most important tasks of any social work organisation.

The book is a practical one drawing on many years experience of training supervisors both in social work and allied professions. It aims to give supervisors and opportunity to reflect on their practice, consider their own supervisory style and how to use well known practice tools within the supervisory relationship. It introduces models to help supervisors focus on the day to day experience of the practising social worker, the effectiveness of their work and supporting practice development and change including in situations where there are concerns about performance. The book is firmly rooted in the idea of the supervisor as the leader of practice and the need for supervision to be ultimately focused on the experience of the service user.

Good supervision is not only the responsibility of the supervisors, it is a joint venture between the supervisor, the supervisee and their organisation, with all having a role to play in making the best possible use of supervision. Although aimed at supervisors, supervisees can also use this book to help them to understand what good social work supervision looks like, and to empower them to demand high standards of supervision within their own organisation.

ACKNOWLEDGEMENTS

The book is dedicated to the late Dr Tony Morrison, who was an inspirational leader in the field of social work supervision and whose thinking has influenced so many of us struggling to find ways to support supervisors in their work. It has been an opportunity to relay to a wider audience some of Tony's work which he set out in the two guides published by the Children's Workforce Development Council (CWDC) to support the supervisors of social workers in the early stages of their professional development. Tony's enthusiasm and commitment has kept many social work supervisors afloat when the going was tough, and in a small way this book aims to provide a point of reference for all of those who use supervision as a tool to sustain social work practitioners in some of the challenges they face on a day-to-day basis. As well as being indebted to Tony for his support and intellectual challenge as my ideas about supervision developed, I would also like to thank all the social work supervisors who have shared their experiences with me over the years and in doing so have been so influential in shaping the material in this book. A special thanks to Linda Gast and Jane Wiffin colleagues at In-Trac who provided such helpful feedback on the manuscript as it progressed.

CHAPTER 1

Introduction – Social Work Supervision in Context

Key messages from this chapter

- Supervision is a fundamental aspect of social work practice.

- At the heart of supervision is a relationship with a supervisee.

- In social work supervision there is a case for reducing emphasis on management processes and increasing emphasis on reflection, critical thinking and emotional support.

- The leadership of practice is a crucial aspect of effective social work supervision.

Why is social work supervision important?

The introduction to this series argued that:

> Good social work involves the capacity to develop and maintain relationships, manage the emotional dimension of the work and make judgements and decisions, often in the light of conflicting information. This is demanding work and will only be effective if social workers are encouraged to reflect critically on their practice and to continue developing their knowledge and skills.

This book focuses on one key relationship: that of the social worker and their supervisor, and is intended to be a practical guide to assist anyone with responsibility for supervising social workers. Since the purpose of the book is to be accessible and practical, it cannot cover every aspect of supervisory practice in depth, and it does not purport to be an academic text. The author is, however, clear about its perspective, which is that the supervisory relationship is fundamental to the delivery of effective social work services, and that there is a direct link between the quality of supervision and outcomes for service users.

A point to consider

- On a scale of 1–10, how far has the quality of your social work practice been affected by the type of supervision you have received?

There are competing specific definitions of social work supervision, and these will be explored later in this chapter, but all are based on the idea of one person working with another within a professional relationship. Social work supervision is therefore essentially a relationship between two people, with the ultimate aim of improving social work practice and outcomes for service users.

Supervision can take many forms, although for many the first thought, when supervision is mentioned, will be the one-to-one session. How to work with supervisees on a one-to-one basis does form the background for much of the content of this book, although this should not be taken to mean exclusively within the pre-arranged, formal supervision session. Ad hoc discussions and establishing a positive culture of supervision within teams are all part of the supervisor's role. Supervisors are supervisees too. The ideas in this book should be just as relevant to the supervision of the supervisor. It is to be hoped that supervisees will also be able to use the book to gain a clearer understanding of what good supervision should look like, and therefore of what they can expect from their supervisors.

The supervisory relationship does not, however, exist in isolation; it will affect and be affected by other relationships. In most social work settings within England the supervisor is not only directly accountable for the quality of individual practice; she is also the supervisee's manager, and acts at the interface of a number of systems which sometimes have competing values, attitudes and priorities. Supervisors are likely to have responsibilities for overall practice standards within their team, meeting the demands of their organisation, and also for maintaining effective relationships with other allied professionals.

The role of the social work supervisor is therefore challenging and immensely interesting. The supervisor needs to see himself, and be recognised by others, as a leader of practice with a key role in promoting the best possible outcomes for the users of social work services. Supervisors need support to do their job, and this book aims to contribute to that support by providing opportunity for reflection, as well as frameworks and tools to help them in their day-to-day work. The book draws on the author's experience of training social work supervisors over a period of 18 years, as well as her own research into the link between supervision and outcomes for service users. It uses an understanding of the interrelationship between supervision, culture, policy drivers and organisational context as the basis for establishing the core principles of effective social work supervision, and for helping supervisors to develop their skills in this crucial aspect of their work. The context may change, and its influence needs to be understood, but the aim is for supervisors to be able to work within the current environment to deliver the type of supervision that is most likely to lead to positive results for children, adults and their families.

Social work supervision in context

The practice of supervision in social work is not new. It has a long history within the profession, although its focus has shifted over time, mirroring the role and function of social work within society and the organisational context within which it operates.

Although there is some debate about the early functions of supervision (Tsui 2005), social work's roots within the charitable sector, with paid staff managing the volunteer workforce, point to supervision emerging first as an administrative task, closely followed by a developing emphasis on education and support. With the increasing influence of psychoanalytic theory from the 1930s onwards, the therapeutic nature of the supervisory relationship came to the fore, along with an understanding of the importance of the relationship between the supervisor and supervisee. The role of supervision was one of support and reflection on casework practice. Debates emerged about the need for supervision for autonomous, experienced professionals, but essentially supervision remained as an integral element in the professional life and development of social workers.

The growth of managerialism in the 1980s, with its emphasis on accountability and performance management, signalled a shift in the style of social work supervision to one of ensuring compliance, practice audit and task completion. For example, within children's services in England, the introduction of targets for completion of assessments within specified timescales, and greater public scrutiny of the performance of local authorities, increased the pressure on supervisors to manage quantity of outputs as well as the quality of practice. Many supervisors have told the author and colleagues during training that, although they wished to use supervision to promote critical reflection and explore the emotional impact of the work, they were not encouraged in doing so. Messages from senior managers, themselves under pressure from government and elected members, were often that the first priority of supervisors was to ensure task completion; hence the audit function of supervision was promoted, and dominated practice in many areas during this period. Within adult services the introduction of care management also had a profound influence on the process of supervision. Here the focus was on the social worker as the organiser/purchaser of 'packages of care'. In many organisations this was no longer seen to be necessarily the role of a qualified social worker, and the focus of supervision shifted away from the relationships, emotional impact and dynamics of the interaction between social worker and service user to a more practical matters of assessment, completion and the management of resources.

The managerialist model therefore took a strong hold, and persisted throughout the 1990s and early years of the twenty-first century, despite a number of dissenting voices and publications which stressed the need for more focus on the containment of anxiety, and on reflective practice (Hughes and Pengelly 1997; Morrison 1993).

The context for this book is the apparent coming together of several factors to move thinking and practice forward in respect of supervision within social work. In many respects this may provide encouragement for supervisors who want to move away from a target-driven approach to the supervision of social work practice.

First, there is growing public concern about the quality of social work practice, often as a result of high-profile inquiries into child deaths. These inquiries have called into question the capacity of social workers to analyse their practice critically and manage complex dynamics, and have suggested that supervision needs to move beyond checking and accountability to a process that helps the worker to 'to think, to explain and to understand' (Brandon *et al.* 2008b, p.106). Lord Laming's report (2009) to the Government following the death of Peter, a young child in the London Borough of Haringey, noted:

> Regular, high quality, organised supervision is critical, as are routine opportunities for peer learning and discussion. Currently not enough time is dedicated to this and individuals are carrying too much personal responsibility with no outlet for the sometimes severe emotional and psychological stresses that staff involved in child protection often face. Supervision should be open and supportive, focusing on the quality of decisions, good risk analysis and improving outcomes for children rather than meeting targets. (Laming 2009, para 3.15)

Second, within adult social work, the move towards personalised services and individual budgets, as well as an increasing focus on safeguarding adults and working at the interface with the child protection system, means that the concept of the social worker as purely a manager of care packages is called into question. Although there is concern that this move will reduce the need for qualified social workers, there is also the argument that social workers operate in an environment where their skills need to move beyond task completion to managing risk within increasingly complex systems.

Third, in England the work of the Social Work Task Force (2009) identified that supervision is an integral element of social work practice that should enable social workers to: 'review their day-to-day practice and decision making, plan their learning and development as professionals, and work through the considerable emotional and personal demands the job often places on them' (Social Work Reform Board 2010, para 2.2).

The principles underpinning the subsequent development of the standards (Social Work Reform Board 2010) for supervision were:

1. That it is the responsibility of all employers to provide social workers with a suitable working environment, manageable

caseloads, regular high quality supervision, access to continuous learning and supportive management systems.

2. That children, adults and families are best supported and protected when employers provide social workers with the conditions above. (2010, p.20)

Alongside the work of the Social Work Reform Board, the Munro review of child protection (Munro 2011b) has promoted the importance of supporting social workers to exercise their professional judgement, and the role of critical thinking as part of this process. Munro's interim report (Munro 2011a) suggested that this might be best delivered by separating managerial and professional supervision. The final report stopped short of this recommendation but has set the direction of travel firmly towards a style of supervision which gives social workers reflective opportunity to think differently and creatively about how best to help the children and families on their caseload.

There is therefore an impetus for rebalancing of social work supervision to include reflection, critical thinking and emotional support alongside the management of practice. This is mirrored elsewhere in the management literature, with an increasing emphasis on the need to understand that, as 'people are the route to performance' (Tamkin *et al.* 2010), building trust, confidence and effective relationships with staff is crucial for success.

Points to consider

- What are the current influences on the way that supervision happens within your organisation? Does it fit with the description above?

- How comfortable do you feel about the expectations placed on you as a supervisor?

- What do your supervisees feel about the current role of supervision within your organisation? Does it meet their needs?

Why supervise?

So far in this discussion there is an inherent assumption that supervision is a good thing and that it will make a positive difference to social work organisations, social workers and service users. In fact, despite supervision being such a core activity within social work, there has been a surprising lack of research into what makes supervision effective.

Tsui (1997) conducted a survey of the published research literature on staff supervision for social workers. All literature published between 1970 and 1995 was reviewed, and only 30 articles or book chapters were found. Of these, 13 involved the supervisor and the supervisee and the rest focused on one or the other of the pair. Consequently, these studies were limited in their discussion of the interactive dynamics of the supervisory relationship. Only two of the published papers (Harkness 1995; Harkness and Hensley 1991) focused on client outcomes.

Hughes and Pengelly (1997) noted: 'Little work has been done on the effectiveness of staff supervision, and little thought given to how its outcomes can be defined and measured' (p.77).

Similarly, Rushton and Nathan commented:

> Very little research has been conducted into the extent, content and quality of supervision and management of child protection social workers, let alone whether it is being used to beneficial effect... No studies have identified methods and styles of supervision that are predictive of a reduction in risk to children. (1996, p.359)

Why is the impact of supervision so underresearched? Tsui (1997) argues that a likely explanation is that staff supervision is embedded within the hierarchy of complex organisations, making the gathering of information a difficult and sensitive task. Other explanations might include the complexity involved in unravelling the huge number of factors impacting on practice at any one time, or the difficulties in designing research based on a term such as 'supervision' which has no clear agreed definition.

Despite the difficulties of conducting research in a complex area, it is important to establish whether supervision does positively impact on practice. As social work organisations struggle to deliver services within tight financial constraints, anecdotal evidence suggests that when time is scarce the quality and quantity of supervision is reduced. Does this indicate that social workers and their managers do not really believe that there is a direct link between supervision and effective practice? If this is the case, it is important to establish the extent to which supervision can (or cannot) influence practice.

Points to consider

- Can you recall an occasion when, as a social worker, you felt that supervision had a direct, positive impact on the way you worked with a service user?
- What happened in supervision to make the difference?

Despite the paucity of research into supervision itself, there are studies into other aspects of social work practice which have increased our understanding of why supervision is important.

Research into the impact of working with violence and aggression (Littlechild 2002; Stanley and Goddard 2002) highlights the value of encouraging social workers to name their fears and anxieties. Without a culture where expressing fear is accepted as a sign of emotional intelligence and strength, rather than a weakness, social workers may be placed in physical danger. A social worker who does not feel able to tell her supervisor that she has very real concerns about the danger posed by a person in the household may be visiting the home alone, in circumstances where at the very least there should be two workers, or office-based interviews should be the norm. Additionally, where fears are not expressed, anxieties may get in the way of either noticing or taking action in situations where an adult or child may be at risk of harm. In these circumstances Stanley and Goddard (2002) equate the position of the social worker to that of a hostage who, in order to manage his fears, appeases the hostage taker. In a family situation the social worker focuses on developing a safe relationship with the violent person and, as a result, may be psychologically unable to recognise risks to other members of the household. Social workers are often blamed for failing to act to protect others, yet if a worker has had little opportunity to explore with her manager her (possibly unconscious) fear of violence, and to develop strategies for working with this, emotion may affect both cognition and action, resulting in a child or adult being left in a situation where they experience harm.

Serious case reviews frequently criticise social workers working with adults with mental illness for failing to notice risks to a child, and recommend better communication between adult's and children's teams. However, there has been little exploration of the quality of supervision received by the social workers working with the adults in the household. Do they, for example, have the opportunity to talk over their anxieties about what will happen if they raise child protection concerns with a parent and explore strategies for working with this? In the words of one mental health practitioner on a training course: 'On reflection I usually arrange to visit mother when the child is not there. That way I do not see anything that I might have to deal with.'

Other research has pointed to the link between supervision and staff retention. Gibbs (2001) in a qualitative study explored factors affecting the retention of child protection staff and found that the quality of supervision was an important factor. The style of supervision that was most likely to help retain child protection staff was one that helped social workers to understand the value of what they did, explored the link between feelings, thoughts and action, and the impact of emotion, and promoted adult learning.

A small qualitative research study carried out by the author (Wonnacott 2004) aimed to understand to what extent supervision had a positive impact on social worker practice and outcomes for children in the field of child protection. Findings from the research (which are explored in more depth in Chapter 3) indicated that the style of supervision did make a difference, and that supervision was most likely to be effective when:

- it took place within a supportive and developmental organisational culture

- the supervisor was aware of his own style and its impact on the process and, whilst ensuring a collaborative approach, took an active role in driving case discussions

- the process of supervision was analytical and included challenge, reflection, management of stress and a focus on emotional competence

- attention was paid to the meaning of communication throughout the system.

The need to attend to organisational culture, supervisory style and the process of supervision moves us towards a dynamic model that recognises the centrality of relationships at all levels within the organisation.

Defining social work supervision

Although we can begin to understand why supervision may be important, if a range of professionals from the health and social care fields were to be asked what they meant by supervision, it is unlikely that there would be a consensus view. Terms such as 'clinical supervision', 'counselling supervision', 'peer supervision', 'consultancy supervision', 'managerial supervision' and 'professional supervision' are all to be found in the literature, yet they are all frequently referred to by the shorthand 'supervision' in day-to-day conversation.

A point to consider

- What is the definition of supervision used in your organisation?

One of the key differences among the various types of supervision is the degree to which the supervisor has management accountability for the work which is being undertaken. As commented above, within social work the most common approach is where the supervisor is part of the management system and shares responsibility for practice standards, being accountable both for their own practice as a supervisor and (along with the organisation and the supervisee) for the standard of social work practice. This approach is succinctly summed up by Bunker and Wijnberg, as follows: 'We view the role of the supervisor as embedded within both the management system and the professional practice system, as a key element in each and an essential link between the two systems' (1998, p.11).

The first UK national guide on supervision in social care (Skills for Care/CWDC 2007) incorporated the notion of accountability and set supervision firmly within a supportive developmental framework linked to service user outcomes: 'Supervision is an accountable process which supports, assures and develops the knowledge, skills and values of an individual group or team. The purpose is to improve the quality of their work to achieve agreed objectives and outcomes' (p.5).

The document goes on to describe three interrelated functions of supervision: line management, professional (case) supervision and continuing professional development.

The definition of supervision as fulfilling particular functions for the individual and the organisation is perhaps the most commonly used definition within the social work literature. It was Kadushin (1976) who identified supervision as consisting of management, support and education and Richards, Payne and Sheppherd (1990) who added the fourth function of mediation. Mediation was described as representing staff needs to higher management, negotiating coordination of services and clarifying the role of the team to others outside the agency. This four-function model was used by Morrison in defining supervision:

> Supervision is a process by which one worker is given responsibility by the organisation to work with another worker(s) in order to meet certain organisational, professional and personal objectives which together promote the best outcomes for service users. These objectives or functions are:
>
> 1. Competent accountable performance (managerial or normative function)
> 2. Continuing professional development (developmental/ formative function)
> 3. Personal support (supportive/restorative function)
> 4. Engaging the individual with the organisation (mediation function)
>
> (2005, p.32)

This definition identifies supervision as a process rather than an event, and involves negotiating complex relationships beyond that of the supervisor and supervisee.

The Social Work Reform Board in England developed a framework for supervision, setting out four key elements:

> Supervision should:
>
> 1. Improve the quality of decision making and interventions

2. Enable effective line management and organisational accountability

3. Identify and address issues related to caseloads and work load management

4. Help to identify and achieve personal learning, career and development opportunities.

(The Social Work Reform Board 2010, p.20)

Beyond a functional model

In summary, much of the supervision literature focuses on a functional model of supervision, describing supervision as fulfilling either three or four functions.

Task

Using the four functions of supervision (Morrison 2005) and reflecting on the supervision that you have received as a supervisee, give each function an average mark out of ten in order to indicate the degree to which that function was regularly addressed during supervision sessions.

Would the marks change depending upon the supervisor?

How would you rate the supervision you give to your supervisees?

Table 1.1 Functions of supervision described in supervision literature

Hughes and Pengelly 1997	Skills for Care/ CWDC 2007	Kadushin 1976	Richards et al. 1990 and Morrison 2005	Social Work Reform Board 2010
1. Managing service delivery	1. Line management	1. Management	1. Management	1. Quality of decisions and interventions
2. Facilitating practitioners' professional development	2. Professional supervision	2. Education	2. Education	2. Line management and accountability
3. Focusing on practitioners' work	3. Continuing professional development	3. Support	3. Support	3. Workload management
			4. Mediation	4. Learning and development

It would not be surprising if, when you reflect on the supervision you give or receive, there is a lack of balance across the functions. Using their three-function model, Hughes and Pengelly (1997) note that:

- it is difficult to address all three functions in any one session

- the interrelationship between the three functions means that they cannot be regarded separately

- supervision becomes unsafe if one function is ignored or avoided for any length of time.

A small-scale qualitative study of child protection supervision (Gadsby Waters 1992) found an emphasis on managerial aspects of supervision, and a similar picture was found more recently when Kadushin's model was used to analyse findings of a survey by the British Association for the Study and Prevention of Child Abuse and Neglect (Bell 2009). Of 113 questionnaires completed by delegates to the 2009 Baspcan Congress, 4 per cent indicated that less than 10 per cent of time in a supervision session focused on support, whereas 39 per cent said that more than 40 per cent of the time was spent on management.

Of the total respondents to the Baspcan survey, 29 were social workers, and of these, rather worryingly, 17 per cent said that they felt supervision was irrelevant, and only 14 per cent said they were 'very satisfied' with supervision, compared to 22 per cent of medical staff.

It is not always easy for a busy manager to deliver the type of social work supervision that addresses all the functions of supervision all of the time, and it is clear that supervision is not perceived by social workers as meeting their expectations. In England the implementation of the pilot support programme for newly qualified social workers prompted some organisations to employ external supervisors, leaving managers to concentrate on management tasks. The evaluation of the first year of the project (CWDC 2010) noted that this could work well, but some social workers noted that roles could become confused and that there is the danger of 'outsourcing reflection' (p.25).

An additional factor to take into account is that social work does not always take place within a social work team. Social workers increasingly work within multidisciplinary environments where responsibility for the work of the team falls to a professional other than a social worker. In such environments it might be entirely appropriate that the social worker's professional supervision is outsourced and delivered by someone who has no managerial responsibility. This model is common in many professions other than social work and can work well, as long as roles, responsibilities and lines of communication are established right from the start.

Definitions of supervision which focus on functions alone therefore have their limitations. The starting point of this book is that good social work supervision must move beyond a functional approach to an integrated model which focuses on the supervisor as a leader of practice. As a leader of practice the supervisor will be concerned about both individual casework and the conditions within which good practice can thrive. Within an integrated approach every discussion about a child, adult or family will involve, to a greater or lesser extent, consideration of the social worker's feelings, their development needs, the quality of their practice and the impact of the context within which they are working. Contextual factors may include, for example, balancing organisational requirements with the expectations of other professionals. The support and development functions of supervision will not be seen as something separate from the day-to-day discussions of practice. There will, of course, be issues that are not case-specific that need to be addressed within supervision, including workload and aspects of continuing professional development. However, a truly integrated approach will automatically ensure that emerging issues from practice, relating to the emotional impact of the work, knowledge and skill gaps, and capacity to achieve the requirements of the organisation, are fed into more general, non case-specific discussions. In addition, the impact of organisational and team context on competence and capacity to make effective judgements and decisions must be taken into account within supervision.

Case study: an integrated approach to supervision

Belinda has just started work in a children and families team, having previously worked in a youth offending team. One of her cases is a family with two children under five and three teenagers, that is well known to the department and has recently been re-referred due to increasing concerns about the mother's alcohol use. The decision has been made to complete a core assessment. Other professionals such as the health visitor are very concerned, and feel that Children's Social Care should not previously have closed the case. A recent departmental inspection was critical of the timeliness and quality of core assessments and there is pressure on the team to improve their performance. Belinda is nervous about the assessment, although she has many years' experience of conducting assessments, since in the youth offending team they use a different assessment framework and she is not sure that her knowledge of child development is up to speed. The family also lives a few streets away from her and she knows they have a reputation for aggressive behaviour.

Supervision in this case will not just be about day-to-day case management, and getting the core assessment done; it must also include:

- attending to Belinda's developmental needs in relation to child development and her understanding of the assessment framework used within Children's Social Care

- emotional support for Belinda and consideration of the implications of working with a family who live close to her home

- acknowledging the possible impact of professional relationships on the assessment process and, where appropriate, mediating across professional boundaries

- making sure that Belinda understands her role responsibilities and organisational expectations

- encouraging critical reflection and analysis of information as it emerges through the assessment process, with a focus on what it means for the outcomes for the children in the family.

In this way all functions of supervision are addressed, supervision focuses on both management and professional aspects of the work and ensures the needs of the service user (in this case the children) remain at the centre.

Critical reflection and social work supervision

Already this chapter has raised the subject of moving towards a style of supervision that encourages a more reflective approach to social work, and has commented on the need for critical reflection within social work practice. Care needs to be taken with terminology here, as 'reflection' is a term which can be overused and under-defined, and a plethora of different theories have developed to explain this aspect of practice (Fook, White and Gardner 2006). Within the context of social work supervision there is a danger that 'reflective supervision' is entering the social work language as a shorthand for describing any supervision that tries to move away from a purely managerial focus. Morrison (CWDC 2009a) helpfully uses the four levels of reflection (Ruch 2000) to explore its meaning and application to the supervisory process. The four levels of reflection described by Ruch are:

1. *technical* – a pragmatic form which compares performance with knowledge of 'what should be done'

2. *practical* – which draws on the work of Schön (1983) and concerns to the practitioner's self-evaluation, insight and learning. This will move from 'reflection on action' (reflecting after the event on what happened) to 'reflection in action', which involves being able to use experience and intuition to respond ' in the moment'. Schon describes this as: 'spontaneous routine behaviour → surprise → attention to surprise → restructuring thinking → delivery of new action as an on-the-spot experiment → observing the effects of the action → getting immediate feedback' (Schön 1994, p.12).

3. *process* – which has roots in psychoanalytic theory and involves awareness of the impact of unconscious processes and intuitive responses on professional judgements

4. *critical* – which acknowledges that understanding can only ever be partial and is continuously evolving, influenced by the social and political context. It encourages the questioning of the influence of power relationships and assumptions underpinning our view of the world in order to inform 'the scrutiny and development of practice' (Fook *et al.* 2006). Reflective practitioners 'possess a rich mixture of normative,

interpretative and critical theory which allows them to continuously question and revise their theories, as well as pay attention to the moral and ethical aspects of practice' (CWDC 2009a, p.127).

The levels do not happen in sequence; at any one time we will be moving back and forth between the levels, depending upon the issue being discussed or the situation we are in. The key for the social worker supervisor is to encourage practitioners to use *all* four levels and to make sure that true critical reflection is part and parcel of the repertoire of social workers and supervisors alike. We have already acknowledged that rarely is the work of the social worker simple; on a day-to-day basis they are working with complex family and professional dynamics and making difficult professional judgements. Critical reflection used as part of the process of supervision is likely to provide a basis for sound analysis, professional judgement and decision making.

The supervisor as leader of practice

An integrated model of supervision requires supervisors to inspire, motivate and act as leaders of social work practice. Really good social work supervisors will not just fulfil the requirements set out in a supervision policy; they will be passionate about social work, interested in developing creative solutions to the day-to-day dilemmas of practice, and absolutely focused on promoting positive outcomes for service users. Besides this they will understand that leading practice requires them to develop the best possible working relationships with those around them, including colleagues and partner organisations. They will have a high level of self-awareness, understand the impact that their own behaviour has on others, and make sure that they have supervision, consultation and support mechanisms of their own.

Given the crucial role of supervision in leading practice, it is surprising that there has been limited integration of the now extensive literature on what constitutes effective leadership with that of supervision. The work of the Social Care Institute for Excellence (SCIE 2009) has focused on the manager as practice leader, and supervision is one of the 11 sessions in their development programme (see Further reading and resources section below). However, this resource is focused on the overall role of management rather than solely on supervision, and more focus on knowledge about leadership and how it can help supervisors is an area for development in the literature, considering that the focus of much of the current work on leadership emphasises the key role that relationships play in effective leadership and positive outcomes. Within social work one such relationship is that between the social worker and the supervisor.

In the UK, research by the Work Foundation (Tamkin *et al.* 2010) aimed to identify how leadership enabled high performance, and what distinguished a good leader from an outstanding one. From 262 interviews a number of key themes emerged which are used to describe outstanding leaders; themes which potentially have much to offer organisations considering what needs to be in place to support the development of social work supervisors. The chart below takes these themes and considers what this might mean for supervisors as leaders of practice. What immediately becomes obvious is that supervision involves working at many different levels, and leading practice incorporates understanding self, the team, the organisation and the capacity to develop and foster relationships at all levels.

A common thread through all of the aspects of outstanding leadership is the capacity to work with emotions. The link between the leadership literature, working with emotions and supervision practice is explored in an extremely useful guide for front-line and middle managers produced in Australia by the Victorian Government Department of Human Services (Gibbs, Dwyer and Vivekananda 2009; see Further reading and resources at the end of this chapter). Entitled *Leading Practice,* the guide explores the dynamic influence of organisational culture, manager capabilities and process on outcomes for children, and emphasises leadership, supervision and management as a primary means by which middle managers lead practice. The interactive nature of leadership style and the process of supervision is explored through the six emotionally intelligent leadership styles identified by Cherniss and Goleman (2001). In summary, these styles are:

- **visionary** (sets standards and maximises commitment to the organisation's goals and strategy)

- **affiliative** (fosters harmony and is in tune with emotional needs of the team)

Table 1.2 Outstanding qualities in leaders and supervisors

Outstanding leaders (Tamkin et al. 2010)	Outstanding supervisors
• think systemically and act long-term. Recognise the interconnected nature of the organisation.	• understand systems and take account of the positive or negative chain reactions which will influence practice in the long term
• bring meaning to life. Enable a strong shared sense of purpose and emphasise emotional connection for people with a focus on passion and ethical purpose.	• focus on the value of what social work can achieve through developing relationships with colleagues and service users
• apply the spirit and not the letter of the law. Focus on how values are communicated – process is a tool to support engagement, not an end in itself.	• use policies and procedures as a framework for good practice, encouraging flexibility and innovation in the best interest of service users
• grow people through performance. See their role as developing, trusting and empowering people.	• value the supervisee's ideas and encourage creativity within a safe environment
• are self-aware and authentic to leadership first, their own needs second. Think about their own impact on their colleagues and consider the needs of the people they are leading.	• access supervision for themselves. Reflect on their own supervision style and consider the impact this has on their supervisees

Outstanding leaders (Tamkin et al. 2010)	Outstanding supervisors
• understand that talk *is* work Move beyond the 'open door' approach by taking the 'open door into the workplace. see opportunities in every interaction and spend time talking and building trusting and positive relationships.	• use both formal and informal supervision to develop relationships, and value the opportunity provided by supervision to talk about practice
• give time and space to others Enthuse others through helping people to focus on key tasks and interpreting and prioritising organisational demands. Give people freedom and influence over what they do.	• provide an appropriate 'buffer' to organisational demands and assist the social worker in maintaining a focus on good practice
• put 'we' before 'me' Invest in developing team spirit and are able both emotionally and practically to allow people to perform rather than 'rescue' to put things back on their preferred path.	• do not let their own anxieties lead them to 'take over' the supervisee's practice • encourage a mutually supportive team environment and learning from each other
• take deeper breaths and hold them longer. Appreciate that failure will happen and can work with failure to provide learning and build confidence.	• develop a relationship with their supervisees where mistakes can be explored in a spirit of learning rather than blame.

- **coaching** (develops others through helping them identify strengths, weaknesses and personal goals linked to the organisational goals)

- **democratic** (focus on collaborative working, managing conflict, involves people)

- **pacesetting** (focus on high standards, meeting goals and pinpointing poor performers)

- **commanding** (takes charge, gives clear direction and expects compliance).

The research pointed to visionary, affiliative, coaching and democratic styles having the most significant contribution to make to positive outcomes, with pacesetting and commanding useful at critical periods, as long as they are used cautiously and flexibly with other leadership styles. Good leaders are *emotionally resonant* (able to read emotions, discuss uncomfortable feelings), and this is most supported by visionary, affiliative, democratic and coaching styles. In contrast, the *emotionally dissonant* leader (unaware of their own or others' feelings, uncaring about distress in the workplace) is most likely to develop from overuse of pacesetting and commanding styles.

The message is that the supervisor as a leader of practice will need to have a range of styles available to her and that at different times one style may be more appropriate than another. The skill is in remaining fundamentally true to leading practice through valuing and working with emotions and relationships, with a consistent focus on outcomes for service users. This will be the focus of the remaining chapters of this book.

Points to consider

Reflect on the five leadership styles described above, with reference to the supervision you currently receive.

1. What is the predominant style of your supervisor? – Rate each style on a scale of 1–5, with 5 being 'very predominant'.

2. How does this impact on you in your work?

3. What message does this give you in your role as a supervisor of others?

Conclusion

Supervision as a key component of social work practice has stood the test of time. Over that time its focus has changed, and there is now an emerging consensus that, while management oversight is part of the role in most organisations where social workers are employed, this alone is not enough. Good social work supervision will provide a relationship where social workers can be challenged to think critically, and supported in a role which involves working at the interface of complex family and professional systems. Supervision is about focusing on and leading practice, in the often challenging environment within which social workers and their supervisors work.

Issues from this chapter to discuss with your supervisor

1. What would my supervisees say about the balance of my supervision across the four functions?

2. What might be influencing my approach?

3. What does working at all four levels of reflection mean for me in my supervision of others? How will we both know that this is happening?

4. How can I use my own supervision in order to develop my role as a leader of social work practice?

Further reading and resources

Gibbs, J., Dwyer, J., and Vivekananda, K. (2009) *Leading Practice. A Resource Guide for Child Protection Frontline and Middle Managers.* Victorian Government Department of Human Services. Available at www.dhs.vic.gov.au.

Morrison, T. (2005) *Staff Supervision in Social Care.* Brighton: Pavilion.

Social Care Institute for Excellence (2009) Guide 27: *Leading Practice – a Development Programme for First-line Managers.* Available at www.scie.org.uk/publications/guides/guide27/index.asp

CHAPTER 2

Understanding the Foundations

Key messages from this chapter

- Relationships are fundamental to social work practice and supervision.
- Past experiences will affect current supervisory relationships.
- A negotiated agreement provides a strong foundation for supervision.
- Supervision needs to provide a forum for consideration of feelings, thoughts and actions.
- Informal/ad hoc/group supervision can be helpful, but formal, one-to-one supervision is at the heart of the process.

This chapter aims to look at some ideas and tools that provide the basis for effective social work supervision, namely:

- a *relationship* where the needs of the service user remain at the heart, success can be celebrated, and difficult issues and challenges can be explored

- a *framework* for understanding the relationship between supervision, social work practice, outcomes for service users and the wider context, including the employing organisation and other professionals

- a *model* to use as the basis for social work supervision, and which can be used both in formal and informal settings

- supervision *structures and methods*, and issues to consider in relation to these.

Developing the relationship

How far is good supervision dependent upon the quality of the relationship between the supervisor and the supervisee? Supervision could be seen as a technical activity which simply requires supervisors to follow a set process and 'tick the box' by recording that these requirements have been met. It is not uncommon for supervisors to report that, in a drive to improve supervision standards, policies and procedures have become prescriptive to the point that agendas are set by the organisation; and it is not unknown that supervisors will be directed to start the session with 'How are you?' Whilst on the surface this may seem to emphasise the importance of a supportive relationship, the fact that there is a perceived need to confine human interaction to a box that can be ticked says much about the dangers of reducing the art of social work supervision to simply another procedure to be followed, rather than recognising that at its heart is a relationship between two individuals.

This book is based on a belief that negotiating relationships is a fundamental aspect of social work practice, and that in doing so practitioners need to look beyond the surface and develop a deeper understanding of the meaning of their encounters with others. The need for this in practice situations has been articulated by several writers, including Ruch (2010) and Ferguson (2005), and the starting point of this chapter is that such practice will be supported by a style of supervision that pays proper attention to the quality and dynamics of the relationship between the supervisor and supervisee.

Why the relationship is important – mirroring supervision and social work practice

The term 'mirroring' (sometimes referred to as 'parallel process') stems from the psychodynamic concepts of transference and counter-transference. These are clearly described by Hughes and Pengelly:

> The term transference is used to denote the range of feelings, conflicts, defences and expectations of relationships projected unconsciously into a current relationship (classically with a professional helper) but originating in other, mostly earlier, relationships. The corresponding term, counter-transference (Heimann 1950), refers to the feelings, thoughts and behaviour

unconsciously simulated in the professional by the experience of relating to the service user especially in response to the latter's transference. (Hughes and Pengelly 1997, p.80)

'Mirroring' is one aspect of counter-transference and is most commonly described as a situation where aspects of the relationship between the service user and the worker are played out within the supervisory session. For example, a social worker who was finding it hard to work with a foster carer who continually refused to allow her to see the children alone 'forgot' to discuss this within supervision, unconsciously reproducing the situation where the children's real feelings had become invisible. Of equal importance is the way in which, conversely, the process of the supervisory relationship can be re-enacted in the relationship between the supervisee and the family. The author's research (Wonnacott 2004) included a situation where a family described their social worker as unnecessarily punitive and not a person they could be open with. Tracking back to the interviews with the social worker and his supervisor, it was clear that the supervisor's style of supervision was very directive and most of her team described her as a bully. The relationship between the social worker and the supervisor was one where he feared getting it wrong and was not able to talk about his feelings of inadequacy in working with this particular family in supervision. Instead, what happened was that in his quest to make sure that he 'got it right' he re-enacted the supervisor's very directive approach in his own work with the family and, in fact, made it less likely that he would be successful in getting to the heart of the issues facing them.

In essence the lack of attention to developing an effective relationship within supervision resulted in the position represented in Figure 2.1.

Authority and the supervisory relationship

The above example illustrates not only the importance of the relationship and its impact on practice, but also the centrality of power and authority within both supervision and social work practice. Is it therefore enough for the supervisor to be a position of authority (either due to his position in the organisation, or vested in them by virtue of his supervisory role) or is it important that time is spent establishing the role, boundaries and the extent of that supervisor's authority?

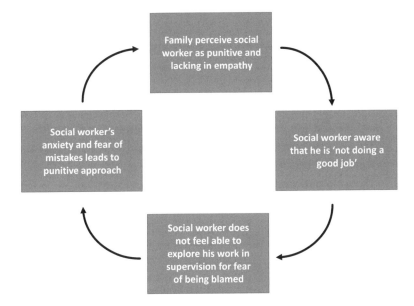

Figure 2.1 Consequence of poor relationship within supervision

Hughes and Pengelly (1997) helpfully identified that the best supervisors will be clear about the nature of their authority and will integrate:

- role authority – vested in them by the organisation
- professional authority – derived from their own professional competence
- personal authority – based on who they are and the way they manage themselves.

This leads to the conclusion that simply relying on role authority is not enough, and that time needs to be spent at the start getting to know the other person within that new relationship. Too often supervisors who have been given a new supervisory role within the team make the mistake of assuming that because they already know their supervisee they can shortcut some of the preliminaries associated with the start of a relationship. They may rely on their personal or professional authority and fail to invest time and effort in establishing the meaning of their new role in relation to the supervisee – a new role that could and should involve challenging aspects of practice in order to develop the critical analysis required for effective social work practice. Research conducted by the author into the link between supervision and outcomes for children revealed the danger in lack of attention to the new boundaries of the relationship. A social worker whose manager had recently been promoted commented:

> This sounds awful, so don't tell Jenny, because I love Jenny to bits and she's a friend, but I don't think there's anything Jenny could have done with me that could have improved the outcomes, because we're too close you know, we're too much peers you know. (Wonnacott 2004)

Conversely, supervisors new to the team might assume that because their role is clear they do not need to spend time establishing who they are and their professional credibility. One social worker in the author's research sample commented:

> I think that it's slightly the fact that we are fairly early on in the supervision process; we haven't got to the point of trust yet where I feel I know him well enough to be really honest about what I feel about a case. (Wonnacott 2004)

It is not too hard to see that if this situation continued there would be very real danger that the reality of the work with service users could 'go missing' from the supervisory process, with the danger that the complexities of the situation could be minimised and decisions made on the basis of false optimism.

Perceptions and use of authority are, of course, fundamental to addressing any concerns about performance, and this will be further discussed in Chapter 5.

Points to consider

- How do you think your supervisees perceive your authority as a supervisor?

- Is it based on role, professional or personal authority?

- How far does this perception differ from supervisee to supervisee?

The supervision history – what does the supervisee bring to the relationship?

Sound working relationships are therefore based on trust, an understanding of each other's roles, and clarity about the boundaries within which the relationship operates. In addition to this, each party may be coming to the process with differing ideas as to what supervision really means. Often our ideas about supervision will have been influenced by our own experiences of being supervised and of supervising others within a particular team and organisational context. It is dangerous for any supervisor to assume that their supervisees will be expecting exactly the same from supervision as they do; even experienced workers will have had differing experiences, which will affect their response to supervision. Too often difficulties in supervisory relationships can be traced back to a failure to spend time at the beginning, getting to know each other and establishing what each expects from the relationship.

Case study

Peter joined a team working with learning-disabled adults six months ago. He had several years' social work experience working mainly in hospital settings. The main focus of his previous supervision had been meeting targets for discharge, and he had very little chance to reflect on his skill development. The culture of the team had been one where mistakes or uncertainties were not openly discussed, as social workers were fearful of being blamed by their supervisor rather than being allowed to discuss their developmental needs. Peter therefore expected supervision to be oppressive in nature and he approached each session with a view to discussing only achievements, rather than areas of practice where he was less sure of his ground.

Peter's new supervisor thought that due to his experience she did not need to spend too much time on the supervision agreement, and asked Peter to sign a pre-prepared document once he had read it and felt happy with its contents. Within a couple of months Peter's supervisor began to be frustrated at the lack of depth to supervision discussions. When asked if he had any issues he particularly wanted to discuss, Peter always said everything was 'fine'. She began to dread supervision with Peter and found herself keeping the sessions as short as possible. Peter picked up on this and took even fewer cases to supervision for discussion than before. Things came to a head when the supervisor was auditing files and began to see a pattern of assessments that were superficial in nature and did not adequately reflect the views of the service user. When challenged in supervision, Peter said that he was finding that his skills in communicating with some of the service users on his caseload were not sufficient, but he had not liked to admit this in case it was seen as a sign of weakness.

- How would understanding of the social worker's past experience of supervision have helped the supervisor?

- How would proper attention to the supervision agreement at the start have made a difference in this case?

In developing the relationship with their supervisees, supervisors need to understand the factors that might be influencing that relationship, one of the most powerful of which will be the supervisee's previous experience of being supervised. (It is apparent from the above case study that Peter's previous experience had a profound effect on his capacity to use supervision and impacted on his relationship with his current supervisor.) One tried and tested way of doing this is to encourage supervisees to reflect on their previous experiences of being supervised. The following is based on the format developed by Tony Morrison (2005) and used extensively by the author and colleagues with supervisors across the UK. It is best used early on in the relationship and can either be used together in a supervision session, or the supervisee can be asked to complete the exercise alone and bring it along for discussion.

A word of warning:

- A supervision history should only be used with the supervisee's consent.

- If you are using it, it is best to use with all your supervisees so that one does not feel singled out.

- Do not rush the exercise, as it may raise a number of powerful emotions.

Developing the relationship – understanding learning styles

If one of the purposes of supervision is to assist the supervisee in learning and developing, it will be important that the relationship is based not only on an understanding of how adults learn but also on the preferred style of the supervisor and the supervisee. Many readers will be familiar with the four learning styles described by Honey and Mumford (2000) and their theory that each of us will have a preferred style of learning. (For a more detailed exploration see Gast and Patmore 2012, in this series.) The four styles are embodied by:

- *pragmatists*, who learn best when they can see the relevance of what is being suggested, will prefer a problem-solving approach and need to understand how things will work in practice

- *reflectors*, who are thoughtful, thinking before taking any action. They will evaluate alternative possibilities and like to make decisions in their own time

- *theorists*, who are logical and like to understand why a particular course of action is being suggested. They feel at home with concepts and models and enjoy being intellectually stretched

- *activists*, who learn best through trying things out and feel comfortable thinking on their feet.

Table 2.1 Exercise to establish supervision history

Supervision history

List your previous supervisors, starting with the most recent. These may include significant figures outside your current profession.	What was it about their style that helped your practice and professional development?	How did you respond at the time? How might this affect your current response to supervision?
	Was there anything about their style that hindered your practice and professional development?	

This theoretical approach to adult learning is used frequently when working with social work students, yet many supervisors report that they have not considered its usefulness in the realm of staff supervision. It does not, however, take too much imagination to realise that the preferred styles of the supervisor and the supervisee could have a profound effect on their relationship and the way they work together, and be the root cause of some relationship difficulties that later become defined as problematic performance.

Case study
Consider the following exchange:

> **Sam** ('activist' supervisor): I see you are getting a bit stuck in your work with Phillip Jennings, and his family have come into the office saying they really are very worried about him. Why don't we go around together tomorrow for a joint visit? Two heads may be better than one and between us we may be able to understand why he is so opposed to moving to a group home and help him to see the benefits. We could try a live supervision approach with you taking the lead and me standing back and offering suggestions to you as the interview progresses.

> **Pat** ('reflector' social worker): I would prefer to think a bit more about the best way of approaching this. Possibly he would see two of us as threatening and I would want to try to understand a bit more what live supervision means and how it might help. Could I speak to someone with whom you have used that approach first and think about it before our next session?

It is not too hard to see that Sam could feel rejected and get frustrated with Pat, seeing her as unimaginative, obstructive and taking too long to resolve a case. Pat, on the other hand, could feel that Sam was taking an overly directive approach to supervision and bullying her into a course of action that made her feel uncomfortable. If they were both unaware of each other's preferred approach this could become a generalised negative view of each other. However, if at an earlier stage in their relationship their different preferred styles had been acknowledged, this should have provided a platform for exploring their different ideas of how best to approach this situation.

Points to consider

- Are you aware of your own preferred learning style?

- Are you aware of the learning styles of your supervisees?

- How might your own learning style combined with that of one of your supervisees impact on the way you work together in supervision?

Developing the relationship – the supervision agreement

If it is crucial to develop a supervisory relationship based on an understanding of role boundaries, the use of authority and what each party is bringing to supervision, the process of producing a supervision agreement provides a focus for this important piece of work. The issues that are discussed, and the way in which the supervisor goes about the business of making sure that an agreement is in place, give the supervisee important messages about what is important and how supervision will provide a safe environment within which to explore complex feelings and ideas. However, the final written document, which is the end product, is all too often the sole focus of the process. In the very worst cases the agreement is a standard form issued by the organisation, which both parties sign after a perfunctory read in the first supervision session. This approach may fulfil a bureaucratic function and allow a box to be ticked that shows an agreement is in place, but it does not provide the foundation for the relationship, or a point of reference if any difficulties need to be addressed.

The reasons why agreements are important are also spelled out by Morrison (2005), who notes that they:

- reflect the seriousness of the activity

- represent a positive modelling of partnership behaviour

- make roles and responsibilities clear

- provide clarity about authority and accountability

- provide a basis for reviewing and developing the supervisory relationship

- act as a benchmark against which supervision can be audited by the organisation.

Negotiating an agreement, according to Morrison, is a process which involves four stages: agreeing the mandate, engaging with the supervisee, acknowledging ambivalence, and completing the written agreement. Agreements need to be reviewed, and so a fifth and final review stage could be added to the overall process.

A FIVE-STAGE APPROACH TO DEVELOPING AND MAINTAINING THE SUPERVISION AGREEMENT (ADAPTED AND DEVELOPED FROM MORRISON 2005)

1. Establishing the mandate – issues to discuss:
   - ✓ What does our organisation's supervision policy say about the nature and purpose of supervision?
   - ✓ What is non-negotiable in the supervision process?
   - ✓ What is negotiable?
   - ✓ What does the supervisor have a right to expect from the supervisee?
   - ✓ What does the supervisee have a right to expect from the supervisor?
   - ✓ What responsibilities do we both have?
   - ✓ What are the boundaries to and limits of confidentiality?
   - ✓ What records are to be maintained, who keeps them and for what purpose?

2. Engaging with the supervisee – issues to discuss:
   - ✓ What have been the supervisee's previous experiences of supervision?
   - ✓ How is the supervisee best motivated/managed in the light of her previous experience?
   - ✓ What are both parties' expectations around the handling of authority – particularly, though not exclusively, in relation to race, culture, gender, sexual orientation and impairment?
   - ✓ What are both parties' values and attitudes in relation to race, culture, gender, sexual orientation and impairment?

✓ What beliefs does each have about the nature and purpose of social work, particularly in relation to the use of authority with service users?

✓ What is the preferred learning style of the supervisee and how far is this in tune with the preferred style of the supervisor?

✓ How does the supervisee react when anxious or stressed? How is the supervisor likely to know the supervisee is stressed?

3. Acknowledging ambivalence – issues to explore:

✓ How will you know when the supervisee is experiencing strong emotions as a result of the work?

✓ What is the role of supervision in exploring uncertainties and feelings of discomfort or anxiety about the work?

✓ It is OK not always to be in control and feel competent to do the job.

✓ How will you resolve any difficulties in working together that cannot be managed within supervision?

4. The written agreement – issues to discuss:

✓ Who is responsible for completing the written document?

✓ Where will it be stored?

✓ When will it be reviewed?

5. Reviewing the agreement:

✓ What has gone well in supervision since the last agreement?

✓ Are there any areas where we have not stuck to the agreement? If so, what was the reason for this?

✓ How can supervision be improved? What can we both do to achieve this?

Points to consider

• Have you completed supervision agreements with all your supervisees?

• Is each agreement personal to that supervisee?

- Where you have been supervising a member of staff for more than a year, has the agreement been reviewed?

A SAMPLE SUPERVISION AGREEMENT
(adapted from Morrison 2005)

Supervision Agreement

Between . . . . **and** . . . . **Date** . . . .
This agreement is the foundation for the development of an effective supervisory relationship. A new agreement must always be completed if there is a change of supervisor.

The expectations of the organisation are set out in the departmental supervision policy and provide the framework for this agreement. Elements of the agreement therefore relate to the departmental supervision policy and are non-negotiable. However, the majority of the document should be negotiated and agreed between the supervisor and the supervisee.

1. Practical arrangements

Supervision frequency: . . . .

Duration of each session: . . . .

Venue:. . . . .

Arrangements if either party needs to cancel a formal session will be:

. . . .
. . . .
. . . .

Availability of supervisor for ad hoc in between sessions will be:

. . . .

2. Content

The process for agreeing the agenda will be:

. . . .
. . . .
. . . .

3. Making supervision work

What does the supervisee bring to this supervisory relationship (e.g. previous work experience, previous experience of being supervised, and preferred learning style)?

. . . .

. . . .

. . . .

. . . .

What are the supervisor's expectations of the supervisee?

. . . .

. . . .

. . . .

. . . .

What does the supervisee expect from the supervisor?

. . . .

. . . .

. . . .

. . . .

Are there any factors relevant to the development of the supervisory relationship (e.g. race, gender, sexual orientation, age, impairments)?

. . . .

. . . .

. . . .

Agreed 'permissions' - e.g. It is OK for the supervisor not to know all the answers...for the supervisee to say he is stuck, etc.

. . . .

. . . .

How will we recognise when the supervisory relationship is not working?

. . . .

. . . .

. . . .

What methods will be used to resolve any difficulties in working together?

. . . .

. . . .

. . . .

4. Recording

Formal supervision sessions will be recorded on the supervision record and placed in the supervisee's file. Responsibility for completing the record lies with:. . . . .

Ad hoc discussions or other information obtained in between sessions relating to staff development or performance issues will also be noted on a supervision record sheet and reviewed at the next formal supervision session.

Any decisions taken in a formal supervision session relating to a service user will be recorded on her file. Responsibility for this lies with: . . . .
. . . .

Ad hoc decisions relating to a service user will be recorded and placed on her file.

The purposes for which the supervision record may be used are:

- audit of supervision practice by senior managers

- evidence in grievance/disciplinary procedures

- inspections and serious case reviews

- evidence within relevant legal proceedings.

5. Any other relevant issues for this agreement

. . . .
. . . .
. . . .
. . . .
. . . .
. . . .

6. Date agreement is to be reviewed:

Signed:

. . . .

Supervisor   Supervisee

Date. . . . .   Date . . . .

Recording

The sample agreement sets out a method that was used in one organisation for managing the recording of supervision and explaining its purpose. Too often conversations with supervisors reveal some confusion about what should be recorded, and in what place, and the purpose of recording becomes lost.

Supervision records need to distinguish between:

1. Case decisions to be recorded on the service user's file. These should set out both the decision and reasons for the decision.

2. The supervisee's individual supervision record. This will include supervision discussions regarding general issues relating to the supervisee. Issues may include support, learning and development needs, performance issues and evaluation of the progress of supervision.

Remember:

1. Service user names should not be included in the individual supervision record, as this is a document that will follow the worker from team to team and may be accessed by others (such as Human Resources).

2. Any actions to be carried out by the supervisor or supervisee should be recorded in the relevant file.

3. Ad hoc discussions between formal sessions should not be lost. Case decisions will be recorded in the case file and both supervisor and supervisee will need to note any other issues that should be fed into the supervisee supervision record. For example, if a debriefing after a visit identified some support or learning needs, these will need to be recorded.

4. Supervision records need to be kept in a confidential place and copies given to supervisees in line with organisational policy.

A framework for effective supervision – the 4 x 4 x 4 model

This model of supervision is based on Morrison's (2005) model. The model was designed to be a practical tool which would help to promote reflective supervision and locate supervision firmly within the context within which it takes place. The model brings together:

- the four *stakeholders in supervision*

  ○ service users

  ○ staff

  ○ the organisation

  ○ partner organisations

- the four *functions of supervision*

  ○ management

  ○ development

  ○ support

  ○ mediation

- the four *elements of the supervisory cycle*

  ○ experience

  ○ reflection

  ○ analysis

  ○ action.

This way of thinking about social work supervision recognises the interdependence of each element, and therefore moves away from a static, function-based approach. Whilst the functions of supervision are part of the model, it promotes a dynamic style of supervision that puts relationships at the heart of the process by using the reflective supervisory cycle to fulfil the four functions and promote positive relationships with key stakeholders.

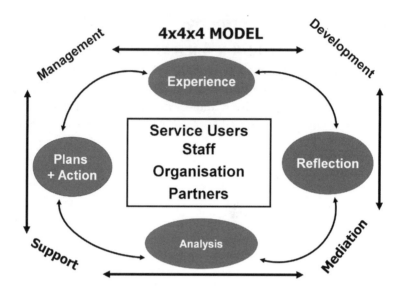

Figure 2.2 The 4 x 4 x 4 model

The supervision cycle

The supervision cycle could be described as the glue that holds the model together. Used as the cornerstone of supervision practice it can have a profound, positive effect on those who have an interest in the outcomes of supervision (the stakeholders) by enabling the supervisor to fulfil the key functions of supervision. It focuses on the detail of practice and its links with the wider system, at the same time as developing an understanding of the supervisees' support and developmental needs.

The supervision cycle was developed by Morrison (2005) from the adult learning cycle identified by Kolb (1988) and, with its base in learning theory, ensures that supervision is a developmental process. This supervision cycle has been extensively used across England and formed the heart of the national training programme for the supervisors of newly qualified social workers (Morrison and Wonnacott 2009). As part of this training programme supervisors were asked to use the cycle with a supervisee and report back on the process. Many powerful stories emerged of the way in which the cycle had made a difference to practice, and on at least one occasion it was clear that, as a result of using the cycle to encourage reflection and analysis, action had been taken to protect a child from significant harm.

Case study

Anna was a newly qualified social worker working in a disabled children team. One of her cases involved Rehanna, an eight-year-old girl with cerebral palsy, who had been receiving regular short breaks for a number of years. This was the main focus of intervention with the child and family, and supervision with Anna's predecessor had usually involved discussion of practical arrangements. In line with the requirements of the newly qualified social worker programme, Anna's supervisor used the supervision cycle to explore Rehanna's situation. During the conversation Anna mentioned that she had a niggling worry following a discussion with the school nurse, who had said that Rehanna had told her teacher that daddy slapped her and shut her in a cupboard. Anna had not mentioned this right away, as she had got the impression that the school thought Anna was making the story up to get attention. This discussion resulted in further enquiries which revealed extensive abuse, and Rehanna was removed and placed with foster carers.

The supervision cycle involves working with the supervisee to understand both the experience of the service user and his own experience of the case as a social worker. It then encourages reflection on this experience through considering the emotional responses of the supervisee to the case, and allows for exploration of intuitive responses and 'gut feelings' about what is happening. Since such feelings will come from somewhere, the cycle allows movement back and forth between the stages, with intuitive responses being further examined in the light of the experiences of the worker. Moving through to the analysis, the experiences and emotional responses are explored within the current context, using knowledge of research and practice wisdom in order to formulate ideas about the main issues that need to be addressed. These are then explored in relation to desired outcomes and what needs to happen next.

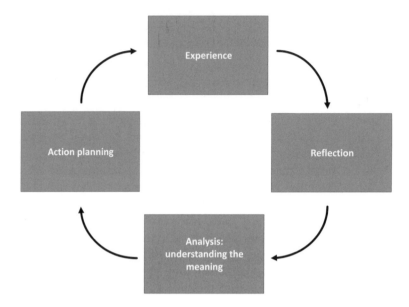

Figure 2.3 The supervision cycle

A detailed explanation of the cycle, including example questions, can be found in Morrison (2005).

WHY DOES THE SUPERVISION CYCLE WORK?

Good supervision will not only make sure all functions are fulfilled, but also will facilitate the full use of a range of knowledge and skills when reasoning about a case. At its heart is our knowledge of the importance of the interrelationship between emotions, thoughts and actions as a secure foundation for decision making.

Too often within supervision, supervisees report that the focus of supervision does not allow for reflection and critical thinking. As one of the supervisees who took part in the author's research commented:

> I would like more of, 'Why were you actually out there, what were you doing, what was the purpose of the meeting, how are you achieving that, what kinds of thought and feelings did you have?' – something that actually challenged me a bit and made me think about my practice. (Social worker in a field work team)

This social worker is describing a type of supervision where the reflection and analytical content is low: a type which is often referred to as the 'short circuit' or 'quick fix'.

Figure 2.4 Quick fix supervision

In this situation the supervisor obtains half a story from the supervisee and immediately jumps to suggestions about what to do next. By moving around the 'half a story-action plan' cycle there is a danger that the rich source of knowledge and skills that the social worker is bringing to the case will be lost.

The cycle allows for exploration of the full range of knowledge and skills that we use when reasoning, as identified by Munro (2008).

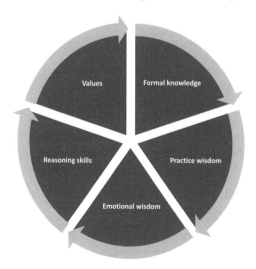

Figure 2.5 Exploration of knowledge and skills in supervision

The supervision cycle provides the social worker and their supervisor with the opportunity to integrate all five factors, based on a thorough exploration of the current experience of the social worker and service users involved.

Case study: using the supervision cycle

Alison is a social worker in a drugs and alcohol team, having transferred there from a community mental health team three months ago. She has been working with Sara for the past two months. Sara is 25, has a long history of drug and alcohol misuse since adolescence, and has previously not wished to engage with any treatment programme. She is now stable on a methadone programme but appears reluctant to talk about any aspects of her life other than her progress in reducing her drug use. She has, however, told Alison she is feeling very positive, as she has a new partner who is very supportive. Alison is aware that Sara has a two-year-old child, Emily. During Sara's last visit to the clinic she told Alison that she might be moving as there had been a fire at her privately rented flat, caused by a faulty electrical circuit.

Using the supervision cycle, some of the questions that might be helpful in supervision are:

Experience:

1. Tell me about Sara – what is your role in this case?

2. What was the purpose of your session with her?

3. What exactly did Sara tell you about the fire?

4. Was there anything that surprised you about what she said?

5. Do we have enough information from other professionals about what happened?

6. What was Sara's demeanour during the session with you?

7. What do we know about Sara's history and her relationship with her new partner and where she might be moving to? I know she has been very reluctant to talk.

8. Have you met Emily? If so, how would you describe her demeanour and relationship with Sara?

9. What did you notice about yourself during the session? Did it go according to plan?

Reflection:

1. What were your immediate feelings when Sara told you about the fire?

2. What range of feelings did you experience during the session?

3. What similar situation have you come across before? What happened?

4. Does Sara remind you of anybody?

5. What are your feelings about children living with drug-using parents?

6. Describe any differences between this session and the previous sessions you have had with Sara.

7. What might Sara have been feeling during the session?

8. What was left unfinished at the end of the session?

9. What feelings were you left with?

Analysis:

1. How would you explain what was discussed during that session?

2. Did the session confirm or challenge your previous thoughts about this case?

3. What evidence is there about the supportive nature of Sara's relationship with her new partner?

4. Is there any information from research into drug and alcohol use that might help us to think about the implications of the information that we now have?

5. What information is missing? What do we need to explore further?

6. What are the current strengths and risks in this situation?

7. How do you see your current role in this case?

8. What are the agency expectations in relation to your role?

9. I am aware that you are new to the team; have you had much experience of working with drug users who are also parents? Is there any support/training that would help you in cases such as these?

Action planning:

1. What are the outcomes that you want to achieve from your work with Sara?

2. What might Sara's view be about what she wishes to achieve through working with you?

3. In the light of our current thinking, what would your summary be of what needs to be done next?

4. What is urgent and essential?

5. What is desirable?

6. How would you prioritise your actions in the light of the above?

7. What support do you need to achieve these priorities?

8. Do we need to involve any other professionals from our team or other organisations?

9. What arrangements do we need to make to feed back on this case?

It is not too hard to see that if the supervisor had quickly heard the outline story and moved on to action plans without a fuller consideration of the case, a number of factors might have been missed, including those relating to the safety of Emily. In fact, in this case Sara's new partner was a powerful individual with a history of alcohol-related domestic violence, and the fire in the flat was caused when Sara and her partner had knocked a candle over during a fight. The social worker had felt some niggles and concerns during the session with Sara, and it was only through skilful supervision that these were articulated and a plan made to liaise with Children's Social Care and the substance misuse team in a neighbouring trust, who were working with Sara's partner.

The four functions of supervision

We have already noted in Chapter 1 that there is some debate about whether we should be referring to three or four functions of supervision. The most glaring apparent contradiction in the English guidance is that between the three functions described by CWDC

Skills for Care/CWDC (2007) and the four-function model, which is part of the 4 x 4 x 4 model (based on Morrison 2005) and was developed as the basis of the guidance used for the supervisors of newly qualified social workers.

The main concern in relation to the three-function model is that it ignores the role that mediation can play in the supervisory process. This is crucial, as mediation plays such an important role in working across the whole system. In fact, such a distinction between the models may be unnecessary, as once the supervision cycle is used as the core process, management, support, development *and* mediation are automatically triggered and feed into the three functions of professional supervision, management and support.

Table 2.2 highlights the interplay between the functions, with the supervision cycle as the heart of the process.

The four stakeholders

The idea of the four stakeholders as part of the 4 x 4 x 4 model stems from the need to describe and understand the impact that supervision can have on outcomes. Stakeholders are those with an interest in whether supervision makes a positive difference, and supervision in itself is only a worthwhile activity if the dynamics of this process can be understood.

Figure 2.6 An adapted 4 x 4 x 4 model

Table 2.2 The four functions of supervision

The four functions of supervision			
Management	**Support**	**Development**	**Mediation**
Professional supervision			
Focusing on the service users' best interest and quality of practice.	Reflecting on the impact of the work.	Self-evaluation and building professional competence.	Ensuring role clarity and effective multi-agency working.
Line management			
Ensuring quality.	Staff care and anti-discriminatory practice.	Managing performance and capability.	Linking to wider performance management objectives.
Continuing professional development			
Identifying knowledge gaps.	Understanding individual learning styles and factors affecting learning.	Providing learning opportunities and completing personal development plans.	Understanding and facilitating external formal learning.

Case study

Southshire is a large county council. The supervision policy within Children's Social Care had not been reviewed since it was first written ten years previously and there had been no supervision training for many years. The standard of supervision across the teams was generally low, with a focus on task completion and little opportunity for reflection, critical thinking or emotional support.

As a result *staff* were stressed, felt that that they had nowhere to go with anxieties about the work, and generally retreated into either risk-averse behaviour (which was interpreted by many *families* as authoritarian and lacking in any understanding of what help might make a difference to their lives), or behaviour that avoided seeing or addressing risks to children. The *organisation* was concerned because staff retention was a major problem, staff morale had deteriorated and a number of serious case reviews had revealed problems in social work practice. The reputation of Children's Social Care amongst partner organisations was low, and professionals spoke either of not wanting to refer into the department because there was 'no point', since little would be done, or needing to take a confrontational approach in order to get referral accepted. As a result relationships and information sharing across the professional network deteriorated.

Although not all the problems with the organisation outlined above will be the direct result of poor supervision, it is likely that the impact of poor supervision is underestimated. Paying attention to improving supervision quality could have far-reaching effects and be one of the most cost-effective ways of turning the organisation around.

Suppose that Southshire decides to review the supervision policy and give a clear message that supervision needs to move beyond performance management to a more reflective, supportive and analytical approach. This is backed up by comprehensive training and support for supervisors, and the quality of supervision gradually improves. *Social workers* feel more able to manage the emotional demands and complexities of the work, their practice becomes less polarised, *families* feel that they are heard, and risks to children are addressed as necessary. Complaints reduce, job satisfaction for social workers increases and staff retention improves. *Partner organisations* feel more confident in the work of the department, relationships improve and there is more dialogue, resulting in more appropriate referrals.

Structures for supervision

One of the advantages of the supervision cycle described above is that it is a way of thinking and can be used not only in formal, one-to-one supervision sessions. Too often supervisors may feel that they do not have time to supervise properly, and therefore retreat to the 'quick fix'. Once using the cycle becomes an internalised response of the supervisor, it can be used in almost all situations. This is important because supervision is a process and, although one-to-one formal sessions should be at its heart, there will be many occasions where supervision discussions take place in an unplanned, informal or ad hoc way (see Table 2.3).

Group supervision

A word here about group supervision, a term which is often used too loosely to describe any group case discussion.

Group case discussions are a vital tool for encouraging critical thinking and can be an important support mechanism within the team, but they are not the same as supervision. Case discussions may be a form of consultation led by an outside facilitator who is accountable for her own practice, but who does not have a formal role within the management structure of the organisation. In group supervision the supervisor is accountable for the standard of work, the well-being of supervisees and decisions arising from discussions. This requires considerable skill in working with groups, and too often supervisors have had very little opportunity to develop and hone their group work skills.

Group supervision can be an invaluable *addition* to individual supervision and is particularly useful in situations where the same group of people are working with the same service users – for example, in residential care settings. However, it should not be a substitute for individual supervision where the focus is on the individual social worker's practice, support and developmental needs. Within a group it is possible for more vocal people to dominate and for some cases to slip through the net. Serious case reviews conducted by the author have on more than one occasion revealed situations where health visitors' only child protection supervision was within a group, and cases that had been worrying them were not discussed due to their perception that the needs of others were greater.

Morrison (2005) gives a comprehensive overview of the issues that need to be considered before embarking on group supervision, with tips for making this a positive aspect of the overall supervisory process.

Table 2.3 Formal and informal supervision

Formal

Formal, planned one-to-one sessions

- Provides consistency, predictability and regularity and is most likely to facilitate the development of a positive relationship. Allows for ongoing review of practice issues linked to supervision records as well as maintaining a focus on developmental needs.

- Beware of relying solely on formal sessions, particularly in situations where there are fast-moving practice developments and decisions which need in-depth analysis may have an emotional impact on the worker.

Formal meeting set up between planned sessions, usually to discuss a specific issue

- Likely to be important in debriefing after incidents or when making urgent decisions. An important aspect of management accountability and support.

- Beware of relying on this form of supervision alone, as it is unlikely to address ongoing developmental needs and may result in long gaps between sessions.

Planned ⟵───────────────────⟶ Ad hoc

Planned informal sessions, such as arranging to have a discussion at the social worker's desk or speaking on the phone after a visit

- May provide support in circumstances where a more formal discussion is not possible.

- Beware of the tendency to fail to record such discussions, particularly if there are issues relating to the supervisee's support or developmental needs that need to be noted in their supervision record.

Ad hoc informal conversations, such as corridor discussions

- May have some limited value in giving a reassuring message to the supervisee that their issues are being heard.

- Generally to be avoided for reasons of confidentiality and likelihood of short-circuiting reflection and analysis stages of the supervision cycle. May lead to flawed decision making.

Informal

Points to consider if you are providing group supervision

1. Are you confident in your knowledge of group dynamics? Have you had training in group work skills?

2. How will you facilitate the sessions to make sure everyone's voice is heard?

3. Have you established the interrelationship between group and individual supervision? How will ideas and decisions from one forum be fed into the other – particularly if you are not the individual supervisor for all members of the group?

4. How will group supervision be recorded?

Conclusion

The cornerstone of all good supervision must be the development and maintenance of a relationship based on openness, honesty and trust. Such relationships do not just happen, and cannot be taken for granted. Supervisors and supervisees will need to find ways of working together to find out about each other, develop a working agreement and constantly be alive to aspects of the relationship that may be helping or hindering the process.

Second, supervision needs to be based on an approach with practice at its heart. This approach will at the same time need to pay attention to the impact of supervision on all the key stakeholders, as well as encouraging the development of the supervisee and supporting him in managing the emotional impact of the work. The 4 x 4 x 4 model on which this book is based is one framework for understanding and working with these requirements.

Issues from this chapter to discuss with your supervisor

1. How effective is the process we use for developing and reviewing supervision agreements? Is there anything that

could make it more effective as a foundation for a supervisory relationship?

2. How can I demonstrate (with you in supervision) the use of the supervision cycle with my supervisees?

3. How can we measure whether my supervision of others is having a positive impact?

Further reading and resources

Gast, L. and Patmore, A. *Mastering Approaches to Diversity in Social Work* London: Jessica Kingsley Publishers.

Honey, P. and Mumford, A. *Learning Styles Questionnaire (LSQ).* Available at www.peterhoney.com

Morrison, T. (2005) *Staff Supervision in Social Care* (2000) Brighton: Pavilion Publishing

- 'Contracts and Structures for Individual Supervision' (p.133)
- 'Supervision and Story Cycles' (p.155)
- 'Group Supervision' (p.245)

CHAPTER 3

The Authoritative Supervisor

Key messages from this chapter

- Supervision style can affect outcomes for service users.
- Authoritative social work practice is important in promoting positive outcomes.
- Authoritative practice is best facilitated by authoritative supervision.
- Balancing a demanding and a responsive style of supervision requires emotional intelligence and an understanding of the emotional impact of social work on the worker.

Supervision and outcomes – the importance of supervision style

Supervision is of interest in as much as it contributes to improved social work practice with service users, and hence improved outcomes. For many years it has been taken for granted that supervision is important, but there has been little precision regarding what type of supervision really makes a difference to practice. The research base in relation to the link between supervision and outcomes is very sparse, with most studies focusing on the interaction between the supervisor and supervisee rather than the connection with positive outcomes.

Within children's social work there has been emerging evidence from serious case reviews (Brandon *et al.* 2008a, 2008b; Reder and Duncan 1999) that a shift in supervision style away from a sole focus on managerial oversight might have made a difference to practice.

Reder and Duncan's study of a year's worth of 'part 8' inquiries noted that supervision should be a 'process of thinking', and Brandon *et al.* commented on their research into findings from serious case reviews between 2003 and 2005:

> These findings add weight to the arguments that effective and accessible supervision is essential to help staff to put into practice the critical thinking required to understand cases holistically, complete analytical assessments and weigh up interacting risk factors. (Brandon *et al.* 2008b, p.326)

Morrison (2005) identifies six factors that link what happens in supervision to the quality of practice. These are:

1. *role clarity*, which involves the supervisor being clear about their role and in turn assisting the supervisee in clarifying her role with service users

2. *role security*, where supervision provides a secure base within which the supervisee is able to explore and resolve confusions and anxieties. This leads to increased confidence in practice and a situation where service users are more likely to trust the competence of the worker

3. *emotional* competence and empathy, whereby the supervisory relationship enables an exploration of feelings, biases and 'mistakes' and models the importance of attunement to emotion in the social work task

4. *accurate observation and assessment*, where the climate in supervision allows an accurate assessment of the worker's competence and encourages a collaborative approach to problem solving which can be translated into the style of work with service users

5. *partnership and power* which is neither collusive nor punitive but enables the supervisee to use his authority appropriately with service users

6. *planning* effectively within supervision, enabling the practitioner to use supervision as a role model to develop clear and shared plans with the service user.

These key factors underpin the link between supervision and outcomes; first, through the style of supervision, and second, through the way in which this style is subsequently mirrored in practice.

The concept of mirroring, also known as parallel processes, was explored in Chapter 2 in relation to understanding why a focus on the relationship is an important foundation for effective supervision. This process has been discussed in supervision literature for many years (e.g. Hawkins and Shohet 1989), but with the emphasis on managerialism within social work, it became less influential in discussions about social work supervision. As explained in Chapter 2, mirroring occurs when the dynamics of the relationship between the supervisee and service user are played out in supervision, or conversely when the dynamics of the supervisory relationship are replayed by supervisees in their work with service users. The process is unconscious and the role of the supervisor is to be alert to this possibility, raise the unconscious to the level of consciousness and use this to explore practice issues. It is vital that supervisors be aware that their supervisory style may be replicated unconsciously in the way their supervisees interact with families with whom they work.

Case study

William was a young, newly qualified black social worker in a team working with learning-disabled adults. His supervisor was a very experienced, older white woman who was under a huge amount of pressure because the team had recently had a poor inspection report. There were numerous instances where she appeared to undermine William's practice by interfering directly and changing decisions that he had made and, because he did not want to increase her levels of stress and anxiety, William did not raise his feelings about this with her. In any case, she appeared more interested in 'throughput' than in listening to alternative points of view or answering questions. The focus of supervision was entirely on whether tasks had been completed and the relevant documentation filled in.

The manager received a complaint about William's work from the family of a young man who said that William had failed to listen to concerns that the young man was expressing about his treatment in a residential unit, and had been more concerned with filling in the review documentation. William had given the impression that the young man's behaviour was likely to be the cause of the problem.

Sensitive exploration of this situation by a more senior manager enabled William to talk about the quality of the supervision he was receiving, the fact that he did not feel listened to, and the focus on completing paperwork rather than detailed discussion about service users. He also thought that there was an element of misuse of power in the relationship, based on gender, class and racial differences. It became clear to the senior manager that William was replicating in his work the style of supervision he was receiving.

Further exploration with the manager identified that at the root of the problem was the level of anxiety experienced by the supervisor, which was affecting her style of supervision. The supervision agreement between William and the supervisor was renegotiated, and during this negotiation there was full and frank discussion about the possible impact of difference and ways in which issues relating to this could be raised in supervision.

Using the concept of mirroring here gives a framework for understanding why the supervisor's style is a key factor in determining whether supervision has a positive impact on practice. This being so, it is important to begin to understand what style of supervision is likely to work best.

A small-scale qualitative study was undertaken by the author into the impact of supervision on outcomes for children on the (then) child protection register (Wonnacott 2004). This involved exploring in depth 27 children whose names were on the child protection register. Following interviews with social workers, their supervisors and the families as well as file reviews, the period from initial to review child protection conference was analysed in relation to the pattern of supervision, the quality of social work practice and eventual outcomes for children. What became clear from the research was that in those cases where outcomes for the children were best:

- the supervisor understood the capability of the worker

- a focus on capability was combined with the capacity to form a positive relationship within a safe environment where difficult issues could be discussed

- the worker's practice could be challenged

- the supervisor was aware of her own impact on the process.

:s of supervision were identified:

e active intrusive supervisor. This supervision style was
iaracterised by a predominantly task-centred approach to
apervision. Supervisors were active in making sure that they
understood their supervisees' cases and made sure that visits
were made, children were seen and reports completed. They
gave little opportunity for reflection and tended not to engage
in conversations about feelings and the impact of the work on
the supervisees.

2. *The active reflexive supervisor.* This type of supervisor also took
an interest in the supervisee's work and was conscientious
in ensuring tasks that were completed as required. However,
they also facilitated critical reflection, challenged supervisees'
thinking and were interested in the emotional impact of the
work. Most importantly, they were aware of their own impact
on the supervisee and the supervisory relationship and were
constantly evaluating their own performance.

3. *The passive supervisor.* This type of supervisor was keen to
be responsive to supervisees and allowed them to define
the supervision agenda. They were unaware of the detail of
supervisees' work, showed little interest in task completion,
provided little challenge and were more interested in ensuring
that supervisees felt supported.

Although a small study, the results made it very clear that there was
a positive correlation between an active reflexive supervisory style
and positive outcomes for children. Neither the active intrusive nor
the passive supervisor managed to create an environment where there
was the necessary combination of critical thinking and support which
allowed effective social work to take place.

The importance of understanding not only the process of
supervision but also the style of the supervisor and his capacity
to manage relationships effectively cannot be overestimated. The
evidence seems to indicate that a process-driven, 'tick-box' approach
to supervision is unlikely to result in the best outcomes for the
recipients of a social work service.

Points to consider

- Reflecting on the three styles of supervision outlined above, which one do you think your supervisees would recognise as your predominant style?

- What are the major influences on your style?

- Are there any aspects of your style that you would like to change? What needs to happen for this to be possible?

Authoritative practice and authoritative supervision

The second serious case review into the death of Peter Connelly in Haringey (Haringey Local Safeguarding Children Board 2009) made numerous comments about the need to act *authoritatively* with families where there are child protection concerns (in, for example, paras 3.8.4; 3.16.7; 3.18.4; 3.20.4; 3.22.2). The notion of the authoritative practitioner has entered the social work language, and it is helpful for supervisors to be clear about what this means, why it is important, and how the style they use in supervision may or may not facilitate authoritative practice. The premise of this chapter is that in order to facilitate authoritative practice, supervisors must use an authoritative style of supervision.

The idea of the authoritative practitioner comes directly from research into which factors are most important in determining outcomes for children and young people. Current evidence (Lexmond and Reeves 2009; Lexmond, Bazalgette and Margo 2010) points to the importance of parenting style over and above structural factors (such as income or social background) as the key variable in determining positive developmental outcomes. Whilst parents experiencing structural disadvantage may be facing particular challenges, and there is evidence that financial poverty is tied to poorer cognitive development (Kiernan and Mensah 2008), children from all income bands display developmental difficulties. Lexmond and Reeves argue that evidence suggests that: 'Parents on a low income but who are confident and able, are as effective at generating character capabilities in their children as parents on high income' (Lexmond and Reeves 2009, p.36).

Using the typology developed by Baumrind (1978), parenting styles can be divided into four types according to the degree to which they facilitate warmth and loving attachments and clear expectations, boundaries and rules. The four types are described as:

1. authoritative or 'tough love'

2. authoritarian

3. laissez-faire or permissive

4. disengaged or neglectful.

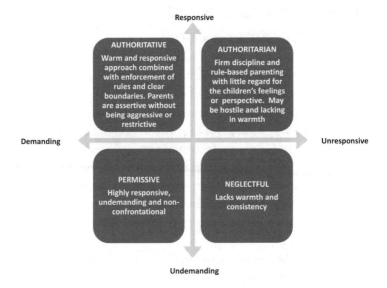

Figure 3.1 Four parenting styles

Although the research specifically looked at parenting, in fact the findings and ideas have applicability wherever there is a caregiving relationship. For example, scandals in residential care environments such as those in the Longcare Home for adults with learning disabilities (Pring 2011) may well illustrate a style of caring that is in the authoritarian/neglectful half of the framework.

What has this to do with supervision and social work practice?

By analogy with parenting styles, it can be argued that the authoritative social work practitioner is one who is clear with service users about expectations and the boundaries, but at the same time is able to show empathy and regard for the service user's perspective

– in short, a social worker who is able to work effectively with relationships. Too often social workers may slip into authoritarian, permissive or even neglectful styles, not generally due to lack of capability but as a result of their own anxieties, or lack of clarity about their role. The task of the supervisor is to work with the supervisee in order to maximise the possibility of authoritative practice.

Case study

Ginny was a newly qualified social worker working in a child care team. She was allocated the McDonald family, who had six children and had been known to the team for several years. The children had all been on a child protection plan, but at the last conference it was decided that there had been sufficient progress for them to be treated as children in need. They had developed a good relationship with their social worker, who was just about to leave the department.

Ginny's supervisor had been off sick, and Ginny had no opportunity to discuss her role with the family before her first visit. She was aware that there appeared to have been drift in the past and was determined to make sure that she focused on the needs of the children. She was very anxious about the visit, especially as she had heard that Mr McDonald had a reputation as a bully. Ginny decided that she should immediately assert her authority and that she should not give them the opportunity to play her off against the previous social worker. She therefore approached the session by introducing herself and being very clear that she was there for the children and to make sure that the positive progress continued. She produced a written agreement which the family signed. This included a list of tasks that they needed to complete. She arranged to visit again in two weeks' time in order to review progress.

Consider:

1. What style of social work practice does this represent?

2. What difference might it have made if Ginny had been able to talk to her supervisor before the session?

One factor that does need some consideration is whether a social worker's role pushes them into a particular style of practice. For example, are social workers in a child protection team more likely to be authoritarian, and those in family support teams permissive? The answer is likely to be that even if individuals strive to be authoritative, the perception by others will be that they adopt a particular style of practice in their work. Team cultures may also develop, which will have a strong pull on individuals within them.

Developing authoritative social work practice – how can supervision help?

The example just described gives a flavour of the potential impact of ineffective supervision on social workers' capacity to remain authoritative in their work. The social worker who is feeling anxious and unsure of her role may well compensate by failing to develop a sufficiently empathetic relationship. She may rush to assert her authority and in so doing forget that in order to develop a relationship, time needs to be spent getting to know the others and trying to understand their view of the world. Ginny, in the example above, did not feel strong enough in her role to risk exploring with the family their feelings about a change of social worker, what had worked so well with her predecessor and what they expected from her. Instead the focus was solely on what she expected of them and little attention was paid to the fundamentals of engagement. Such an approach was likely to result, at best, in compliance rather than real change. An alternative scenario might have been that Ginny's anxiety and role confusion led her to abdicate all responsibility and join the parental system, to the extent that she completely lost focus on the child.

Another factor that is important in relation to supervision is that we will all have had experiences of parenting styles that are likely to affect our response to supervision. For example, a supervisee whose primary experience of parenting is authoritarian may well expect to be told what to do, and find a more responsive/facilitative approach irritating.

Similarly, the supervisee whose experience has been mainly permissive may react badly to instruction and demands. The issue is about recognising that we are not all the same, that our experiences will affect our reactions, and that where irritations begin to emerge, the first port of call is to try to explore and understand these from each other's point of view.

Points to consider

How might your experience of parenting affect your response to your own supervisor when they are:

- making demands of you?

- encouraging you to exercise greater autonomy in decision making?

The authoritative supervisor

The authoritative supervisor is not a million miles distant from the active reflexive supervisor, who was found to have a positive impact on outcomes for children. The style that makes a difference is one where there is a balance between demand and responsiveness, and a crucial capability is the capacity to maintain this balance.

What does authoritative supervision look like?

The authoritative supervisor will:

- be clear with supervisees about expected practice standards and ensure that these are met

- be sure to access the tools they need to do the job (procedure documents, recording frameworks, access to relevant research and literature)

- provide a safe environment for supervision, based upon a mutually agreed supervision agreement which makes clear the negotiable and non-negotiable aspects of the relationship

- be interested in supervisees' practice experience and work with them to critically analyse their work

- take care to understand supervisees' preferred learning styles and will work with supervisees to make sure they have the knowledge and skills to do the job expected of them

- be open to hearing how the work is impacting emotionally on the supervisee

- use their own supervision to reflect on the dynamics of their supervisory relationships.

Figure 3.2 shows the possible outcomes associated with each supervision style.

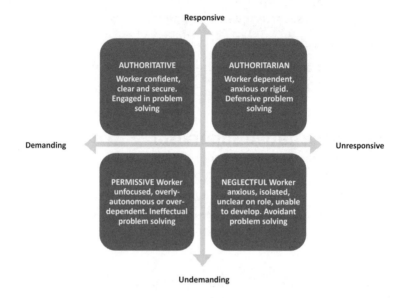

Figure 3.2 Possible outcomes of the four styles of supervision

Points to consider

- To what extent does your supervision style generally reflect the features of authoritative supervision?

- What helps you maintain this approach?

- What gets in the way of an authoritative style of supervision?

- Is there anything you can do to maximise the possibility of authoritative supervision?

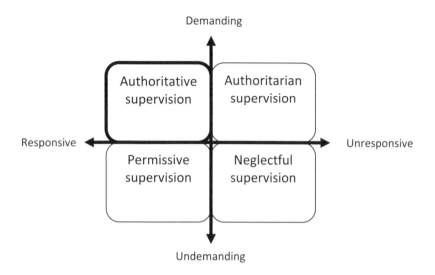

Figure 3.3: Staying in the authoritative zone

Since the least promising of these styles, the neglectful style, is at the outer limits of competent supervision and will be the most obvious to all concerned, the most immediate challenge is to consider the boundaries surrounding the authoritative style and understand what difference makes it likely that the supervisor will deliver authoritative, rather than authoritarian or permissive, supervision. It is likely that from time to time the supervisor will be temporarily pushed or pulled across the boundaries with few negative consequences. However, if the predominant style is authoritarian or permissive and then becomes entrenched, or even moves towards neglectful, it is likely that there will be a negative impact on practice. How, therefore, might the authoritative supervisor remain firmly within the authoritative zone, and what might be the pressures at the boundary?

AUTHORITATIVE/PERMISSIVE SUPERVISION

Where the boundary between authoritative and permissive supervision is being breached, the supervisor reduces organisational and professional demands and expectations, and increases his response to the supervisee's needs and demands. The result here is likely to be a supervisee who becomes increasingly either autonomous or dependent.

Excessive autonomy and dependency, of course, have their dangers, with the overly autonomous practitioner being less likely to use supervision to reflect critically on her practice, and possibly missing the opportunity to see where her personal biases or emotional responses may be affecting decision making. At its extreme, behaviour may become increasingly maverick and at odds with the direction of the organisation as a whole.

On the other hand, the supervisee may become extremely dependent, due to anxiety about not knowing what is expected of him. This may result in either a fractious relationship with the supervisor, who becomes increasingly frustrated by the demands made by the supervisee, or a situation where there is insufficient role security for the development of appropriate professional autonomy.

The issue is how far the supervisor is able to maintain a clear focus on what is expected of the social worker. A number of factors may affect the boundary here, including the following:

- Clarity of expectations within the organisation as a whole – is there a clear performance management framework? Are there mixed messages about priorities and expectations?

- Is the supervisor confident about the evidence-base that informs this area of practice, and confident enough in her role as a supervisor to admit she has knowledge gaps and to agree the action that needs to be taken to make sure that practice is sound?

- How comfortable does the supervisor feel in exercising his authority as a supervisor? Are there other factors that might be impacting on this, such as having been recently promoted within the same team? Is the supervisee more experienced than the supervisor?

- Issues in the individual relationship with this particular supervisee, such as personal friendship.

Game theory (Berne 1964) also provides a framework for understanding interactions that may affect the boundary between authoritative and permissive supervisory practice. Games in supervision were first identified by Kadushin (1968, 1976) and relate to those (usually) unconscious interactions between supervisor and supervisee that will ultimately have a payoff for one of the parties involved. The most frequent purpose of games will be to manipulate demand levels, redefine the relationship, reduce power disparity or increase control of the situation. A variety of organisational and personal factors will impact on the likelihood and extent of game playing. (For further explanation see Cousins 2010 and Morrison 2005.)

At the boundary between authoritative and permissive supervision styles, various games may exert a 'push-and-pull' effect and influence the predominant style of supervision. Table 3.1 shows a few examples.

AUTHORITATIVE/AUTHORITARIAN SUPERVISION

The boundary between authoritative and authoritarian supervision is particularly significant in relation to the degree to which the supervisor is able to engage with and respond to emotions in supervision. Where the boundary is weak it is likely to result in the supervisor focusing on demands, expectations and outputs, with little willingness to see the world from the supervisee's point of view, particularly in relation to the emotional impact of the work.

Factors affecting the boundary here are likely to include an interrelationship between:

1. organisational stress and anxiety and how this is managed

2. individual stress and anxiety and how this is managed

3. recognising the legitimacy of emotions, and ability to work with them in supervision.

The significance of lack of engagement with the emotional content of communications within supervision should not be underestimated, as emotions will influence judgements, and ultimately service user outcomes. Sadly, many social workers may report that in their work environments, anxiety and emotions are not tolerated. One social worker interviewed as part of the author's research (Wonnacott 2004) was clear that their supervisor was not interested in talking about feelings and that doing so would, in fact, be interpreted as a sign of weakness:

> Highlighting those issues is sometimes almost like admitting weakness, and I know it isn't, and they wouldn't say that up front, but it feels like that. I think, perhaps, there could be more probing – you know, are you sure you're OK, how do you feel about this, how did you feel when that happened? (Wonnacott 2004)

Table 3.1 Game theory and supervision

Game	Possible influences	Effect on the boundary
'Treat me, don't beat me.' The supervisee prefers to expose herself rather than her practice and shifts the focus of supervision to personal issues affecting her work.	Supervisor wants to be liked and is not getting effective supervision for himself. Newly promoted supervisor who is not yet secure in her professional identity as a supervisor.	Demands are reduced. Expectations are lowered. Pull towards permissive supervision.
'You and I against the organisation.' Either the supervisor or the supervisee encourages mutual distrust of the organisation, and supervision becomes focused on how to work *despite* the organisation, rather than with it. The supervisee uses the game to deflect any criticism of his own practice.	Poorly managed organisational change. Supervisor who is poorly supervised by his own manager and uses the supervisee as a source of support. Supervisee who feels out of her depth and anxious about the work.	Organisational demands and expectations are deemed to be inappropriate and can therefore be ignored. Both push and pull towards permissive supervision.
'We are too busy for supervision today.' Either the supervisor or the supervisee does not wish to address difficult practice issues, so regains control by cancelling the session.	Organisational expectations and frameworks for managing practice are unclear and the supervisor feels unsure about his role and authority. Organisational culture of blame rather than learning means that *either* the supervisee is worried about consequences of practice discussions, *or* the supervisor wishes to protect the supervisee by not exposing any practice deficits.	Significance of demands and expectations is minimised. Push and pull towards permissive supervision.

Case study

Samuel is a 22-year-old disabled man of Caribbean Black heritage. Samuel has a severe learning disability, no verbal communication and is a wheelchair user due to his physical impairments. He lives with his parents. His mother is his main carer and she provides all his personal care. There has been a history of conflict between Samuel's mother and adult services over the provision of support, and a number of social workers, managers and carers have been physically threatened. Many care providers have refused to continue working with the family, which has led to a high turnover of carers and, at times, gaps in provision. Samuel's mother has also withdrawn him from the college course he was on, which means he spends large amounts of time at home with little or no stimulation or contact with anyone outside the family. The social worker, a white male who has only recently qualified, and who spends all his time trying to make some provision for support to the family and negotiating with providers, is exhausted by the demands of Samuel's mother and has recently admitted to dreading her calls.

Consider:

1. What factors might be affecting the social worker's response in this case?

2. How might the emotional impact of this case affect the social worker's capacity to assess and respond fully to Samuel's needs?

3. What does the supervisor need to do?

In the case just described, supervision discussions initially focused on exploring strategies and plans for managing the provision of services, and the supervisor became increasingly directive and irritated by the social worker's apparent reluctance to confront Samuel's mother. A turning point in the case occurred when, following a change of supervisor, supervision included an exploration of the worker's emotional response to working with Samuel's mother. This triggered the identification of safeguarding concerns that had been previously overlooked, in relation to her care of Samuel.

The case study demonstrates the interrelationship between organisational stress (managing resources), individual stress (working with complex relationships) and the capacity of the supervisor to be responsive as well as demanding, and so remain within the boundaries of authoritative supervision.

What do we mean by stress?

There are numerous definitions of stress in the literature and many reports of social workers being at particular risk of stress and burnout (see www.communitycare.co.uk/static-pages/articles/Social-work-stress).

A full exploration of stress in social work can be found in Davies (1998), which describes stress as a state where the anxiety that is an intrinsic part of social work is not recognised and understood. Another particularly useful definition is that written from a social work perspective by Pottage and Evans (1992). From their research with social work teams they describe work-based stress as: 'a state of permanent heightened anxiety, where the sufferer experiences work as personally threatening, and where the means for reduction of anxiety appear not to be available' (Pottage and Evans 1992, p.11).

The importance of this definition is that it challenges the supervisor to be aware of the impact of anxiety associated with social work practice and to differentiate between anxiety which may be functional (i.e. just sufficient adrenalin flowing to motivate) and anxiety which is dysfunctional, causing the supervisee to be in permanent fight–flight mode and therefore unable to tolerate the uncertainty that is part and parcel of everyday social work practice. The authoritative supervisor is responsive enough to be able to distinguish between the two, and to provide the right amount of support to prevent the slide towards stress from damaging the worker, the team, the organisation and the service user.

Working with stress therefore requires understanding of the impact of anxiety on organisations, teams and individuals. The seminal work of Isobel Menzies, which explored the high level of stress and anxiety amongst nurses, concluded that: 'the success and viability of a social institution are intimately connected with the techniques it uses to contain anxiety' (1960, p.118).

Where anxiety is not contained, primitive defence mechanisms will be used to help the individual or organisation cope, and these are unlikely to improve the quality of the service. So, for example, patients become dehumanised and are referred to by their condition rather than by who they are, feelings are denied, and the weight of responsibility for decision making is reduced by checks and counter-checks. The social worker whose supervisor is also caught up in a situation where anxieties are not contained is unlikely to receive the responsive, authoritative supervision needed. Being responsive and managing stress is not, therefore, a simple linear approach in which either the supervisor or the supervisee changes their behaviour; it requires an understanding of the impact of anxiety at all levels and the flow of stress through the system.

ORGANISATIONAL AND INDIVIDUAL STRESS – A WHOLE SYSTEM APPROACH

Brown and Bourne (1996) outline a model describing the flow of stress through the social work system. In an adapted representation of the model below, the 'ball of stress' consists of the social and political pressure that surrounds social work organisations and professionals. The pressure to get it right all the time and to increase quality with ever diminishing resources pervades the whole system. This will increase stress on teams and individuals, who may well be experiencing stress of their own due to the nature of the work or other factors. For example, team dynamics may be problematic, and an individual social worker may be carrying a caseload that is particularly emotionally demanding at the same time as experiencing stress in her personal life. Underperforming teams or individuals will increase stress on the organisation. In this way the stress ebbs and flows throughout the system and the size of the ball will increase or decrease, depending on how well stress is managed at all levels.

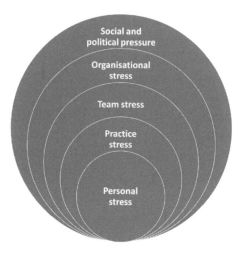

Figure 3.4 The 'ball of stress'

The supervisor as mediator in this system needs to understand the interaction between the various parts of the system, and to be able to work with his supervisee to identify where stress is located, its impact on the supervisee, and what is within the supervisor's or supervisee's control and what is not. For example, in a situation where a supervisee is overwhelmed because of deadlines, and is feeling 'put upon' by the team, it is likely that the supervisor can do little about the deadlines but *can* address some of the negative team dynamics and review the fairness of the worker's caseload.

STRESS MAPPING

Think of a situation where you have described yourself as stressed at work. The following exercise is designed to help you to reflect on the primary origins of the stress and what can be done to help. Consider the possible sources of the stress and tick the box that best describes the impact that each factor has had on causing you to feel stressed.

As stress flows through the system, the extent to which it impacts on practice will depend on the capacity of the organisation and individuals within it to work effectively with anxiety. One model that addresses the link between the management of anxiety and practice is that of 'the collaborative or compromised cycles' (Morrison 2005). Often referred to as the 'red' and 'green' cycles, this model has been extensively used to train social work supervisors across England (Morrison and Wonnacott 2009a). The 'red cycle' refers to a compromised environment where anxieties are not managed and uncertainties are not tolerated. The result of this situation is that the organisation or individual is in permanent 'fight–flight' mode; practice becomes defensive and risk-averse, and there may be conflict with partner organisations.

In the contrasting 'green' cycle there is a collaborative environment where anxieties and uncertainties are acknowledged, any mistakes are seen as opportunities for learning, new ideas are encouraged, diversity is valued and there is cooperation and persistence in searching for shared solutions.

Table 3.2 Stress mapping

Source of stress	High impact	Medium impact	Low impact	No impact	How does this affect my work and others? What can be done? Who can do it?
Factors external to the organisation (Government/media)					
Factors within the organisation (systems, processes, culture, resources, workload)					
Factors within the team (dynamics, sickness, team workload)					
Practice issues (1) Nature of the work (complexity, workload, lack of resources or training to do the job)					
Practice issues (2) Emotional impact of the work (personal response)					
Personal issues (stress in personal life impacting on work)					

Figure 3.5 The 'red' and 'green' cycles (adapted by Tony Morrison from Vince and Martin 1993)

Organisations, teams and individuals may all be operating in either of these two cycles, and may move back and forth between them at various times. What is important here in relation to supervision is that where 'red cycle' behaviour is predominant, the effectiveness of the process will be compromised. The highly anxious, defensive social worker is unlikely to be able to articulate a comprehensive account of the case in supervision or to be honest about his feelings, or open to new thoughts, ideas and ways of working.

In the next example (Figure 3.6) supervision lacks responsiveness to the social worker's anxieties about working in a situation where there are concerns about sexual abuse and violence within a middle-class family. The social worker feels unable to tell the supervisor that she is unclear about her role, and is worried about how to carry out the assessment. This compromises the work she does within the family, what she observes and her capacity to remain authoritative. The assessment is therefore compromised.

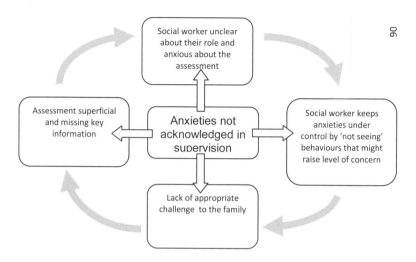

Figure 3.6 The compromised assessment

Emotionally intelligent supervision

Emotional intelligence is one way of understanding the difference between authoritative and authoritarian supervision. The idea of emotional competence or emotional intelligence has been around in the management literature for some time (Goleman 1996) and has more recently gained currency within social work (Howe 2008; Morrison 2007).

Howe describes the emotionally intelligent social worker in the following way:

> The emotionally intelligent social worker recognises the emotional nature of her work and the emotional impact that it has on the self and others. It is in the intelligent use of emotions and understanding of the part that emotions play in all our lives, that effective practice and psychological wellbeing occur. (2008, p.195)

Similarly, the emotionally intelligent supervisor could be described as a supervisor who is attuned to the emotional impact of social work, and able to recognise and manage her own emotional responses so as to be able to recognise and respond to the emotional content of discussions with supervisees.

The emotional intelligence paradigm as depicted by Morrison can help to make clear the difference between the authoritative and the authoritarian supervisor.

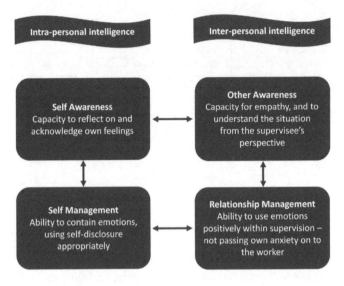

Figure 3.7 The emotional intelligence paradigm and authoritative supervision

Conclusion

Working with emotions in supervision is not an added extra; it is fundamental to facilitating good practice and outcomes for service users, social workers and supervisors alike.

Issues from this chapter to discuss with your supervisor

1. What is my predominant style of supervision?

2. What influences my style, taking account of

   ✓ the function of our team within the organisation

   ✓ my own background and experience

   ✓ current relationships with my supervisees?

3. Thinking about the 'red' and 'green' cycles –

   ✓ Where is the organisation?

   ✓ Where is our team?

   ✓ Where am I?

4. Is there any evidence that my supervisees are experiencing stress? How might I manage this better? (The stress manager competency indicator tool www.hse.gov.uk may be useful here.)

5. How might I be confident that my supervisees feel comfortable discussing their anxieties in supervision?

Further reading and resources

The Health and Safety executive (www.hse.gov.uk) provides a number of tools that supervisors and their organisations may find useful in evaluating how well they understand and work with stress, including measures against the six key standards relating to:

1. demands (workload, work patterns and the work environment)
2. control (how much say people have in the work they do)
3. role (role clarity and role conflict)
4. support (emotional and practical)
5. change (how well this is managed).

Morrison, T. (2005) *Staff Supervision in Social Care*. Brighton: Pavilion.

- Chapter 2 'Supervision and Outcomes in a Turbulent World.'
- Chapter 8 'Emotional Impact: Sources and Strategies.'
- Morrison, T. (2007) 'Emotional intelligence, emotion and social work: Context, characteristics, complications and contribution.' *British Journal of Social Work 37*, 245–263.

CHAPTER 4

Supervising Social Worker Assessments

Providing the Foundations for Effective Practice

Key messages from this chapter

The quality of supervision will directly affect the quality of assessment, and consequently the effectiveness of interventions with service users. The good supervisor will:

- use supervision to promote analytical thinking

- work with supervisees to explore the dynamic relationship between professional systems

- understand that the positive use of emotion is critical to forming judgements and making decisions

- interrogate the meaning and impact of communication

- consider how his supervisory style may impact on the effectiveness of the assessment process

- use tools that help her to understand the unique features of each assessment.

Supervision and assessment in social work

The supervision of assessment includes how workers engage and communicate with service users; how they collect and analyse information and use this to formulate plans; how they carry out and review interventions; how they work with partner agencies; and how they reflect on, and learn from, these experiences.

Assessment is at the heart of social work practice and is not a stand-alone event, but part of the social work intervention with service users. Through the assessment process social workers lay the foundations of the helping relationship, and work with service users to identify areas where change is needed. It is through the skill of the social worker at this point that the very process of change may begin. Quality of practice includes the capacity not only to gather and analyse complex information, but also to engage with sometimes difficult emotions. How well this is handled during the assessment can make the difference between positive engagement and change, and an assessment which only superficially addresses important issues. It is therefore vitally important that supervision of the assessment process fully engages with all the conscious and unconscious processes that are influencing practice at this point.

The last chapter explored the link between supervision, social work practice and outcomes for service users. At the heart of the link is the capacity of the supervisor to understand and work with relationships and emotions and, since assessment is a fundamental aspect of social work practice, this must be at the core of the supervision of assessment work.

It is, in fact, in the supervision of assessment practice that the negative effect of the false separation of supervisory functions becomes particularly apparent. A focus on management tasks may miss an engagement with the intuitive responses and unconscious processes affecting the assessment, whereas focus on support and development may fail to address the purpose and outcome of that particular assessment and the accountability of the supervisor for effective decision making and planning. The mediation role is particularly important, as assessments operate at the interface between the organisation and other agencies involved with the family, and there may be issues to resolve in relation to thresholds, relationships and resources. In every aspect of the assessment process the need for supervision which addresses the interplay between emotions, thoughts, judgements, decisions and the capacity for effective, relationship-based practice cannot be overestimated.

Case study

Jon is an experienced social worker. After working for a short time as a newly qualified worker in a child care team, he has spent ten years working in adult mental health and has recently moved to work in an assessment team in Children's Services. The team manager is very pleased to have an experienced worker, as most of the team are newly qualified and there has been a threefold rise in referrals recently.

Jon has been allocated a case requiring an initial assessment where the mother has been diagnosed with severe postnatal depression and there are concerns about her capacity to care for the baby and four-year-old twins. Her partner has recently left the family home.

The supervisor assumes that as Jon is an experienced mental health worker, he should feel confident in working with this case. In fact, Jon's knowledge of child development is limited and he wishes to develop his skills in communicating with children. However, there have been no learning and development opportunities available to him since he joined the team.

It is not too hard to see that there is a danger that Jon could be anxious in his new role and retreat into his comfort zone of working primarily with the mother, without fully exploring the impact of her mental health on the children. He may feel that as an experienced social worker he should be able to cope, resulting in a reluctance to worry his supervisor, as the team is under a lot of pressure. He could feel de-skilled in relation to his knowledge of child development and ability to communicate with children, resulting in little analysis within the assessment as to what life is like for them. Consequently, judgements could be skewed, the voice of the child lost and interventions may not meet the children's needs.

The good supervisor will not only focus on his management role of ensuring that the required tasks are carried out in relation to the assessment process, but will also ensure that Jon's feelings are acknowledged and he is allowed to explore ways of addressing any knowledge and skill gaps.

Through effective supervision of this one case the supervisor will be able to:

- ensure the team delivers a competent service

- assess the quality of Jon's practice

- explore Jon's feelings about his change in job role a. emotional impact of this on his decision making

- identify and address any learning and development needs.

Throughout this chapter the focus is therefore on using supervision to work with the assessment process at three levels:

1. *psychological* – including the impact of emotions on analysis and decision making

2. *analytical* – evidence-informed understanding of the meaning of information

3. *practical* – competent task completion, risk management and intervention.

Supervisors will need to be familiar with the now growing literature on social work assessments (see 'Further reading and resources' at the end of this chapter). The aim of this chapter is to explore the implications of this literature for supervision and provide a framework for supervisors to use in their day-to-day practice.

The following are some of the critical issues with social work assessments that supervisors will need to consider:

- moving beyond information gathering to analysis

- involving service users effectively within the assessment process

- the impact of bias on assessment and decision making

- integrating intuitive and analytical thinking

- the impact of relationships within the professional network

- developing outcome-focused plans.

In supervising assessment practice supervisors therefore need to operate at the interface of a number of different systems.

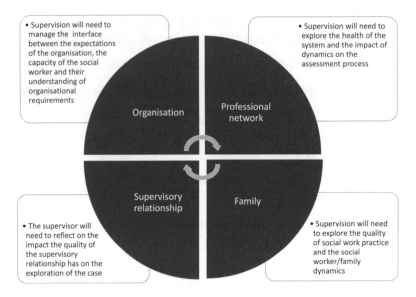

Figure 4.1 Supervision at the interface

Fundamental to the supervision of assessment will be the shared understanding of the supervisor and supervisee regarding the very nature of the assessment process itself and how this links with the organisation's overall approach to the social work task. An important factor here is the quality of professional discretion and authority, and how far the assessment process is driven by the requirements of the organisation or the needs of the service user.

There is a growing recognition of some of the negative effects of the new public management on social work practice (Munro 2011b). Although this may have resulted in greater consistency and opportunity for performance management, its focus on the processing of cases rather than the quality of practice has led to a situation where assessments may be undertaken because a social worker is procedurally required to do so, rather than as the result of a professional decision, ideally taken in conjunction with the service user, that an assessment is necessary. Where the procedural approach is mirrored in a style of supervision which focuses on tasks and process at the expense of reflection and critical thought, it is unlikely to provide a space where the uniqueness of each assessment is recognised and there is clarity about the questions that need to be answered by *this* assessment at *this* point in time.

Supervisors may find it helpful to use with their supervisees the framework discussed below, adapted from that set out in Part One of the Munro review (2010b), to consider their overall approach to the assessment process – that is, are they operating from an atomistic or a holistic approach to assessment?

The six-stage model

The six-stage model for the supervision of assessment practice developed by Tony Morrison (Morrison and Wonnacott 2009a) will form the basis for much of the rest of this chapter. This model was used as part of the framework for supporting and training the supervisors of newly qualified social workers in England and has been used successfully across both adults' and children's services. The slightly adapted version presented in this chapter (see Figure 4.2) aims to provide a framework for supervision that (a) addresses the critical issues with assessment outlined above, and (b) achieves a 'balance of abstract analysis and consideration of human relations' (Munro 2010b, p.16, para 1.21), as well as (c) ensuring that the assessment is based upon the sound foundation of high-quality information and provides a springboard for effective planning and intervention. The model therefore enables the supervisor to address the psychological, analytical and practical elements of the assessment process.

The six-stage model develops the reflective supervision cycle and expands it, focusing supervision on the interrelationship between the assessment process and the dynamics influencing practice. It is presented as a series of interlocking circles with two-way arrows, signifying the cyclical nature of the process and the inevitable moving back and forth between stages that will happen as the assessment develops.

Table 4.1 The atomistic versus the holistic approach to assessment

	Atomistic approach	Holistic approach
Nature	• narrow: tending to concentrate on individual parts or elements	• broad: elements seen as standing in relation to each other
Perspective	• isolated 'problems'	• whole system
Cause and effect	• looking only at immediate and/or proximal effects • short chains of causality	• separated in space and time • long chains of causality, ripple effects; unintended consequences, feedback effects
Style of recommen-dations	• regulation and compliance • technocratic	• strengthening professionalism • socio-technical
Results	• narrow range of responses to service users' needs • defensive management of risk • command and control management; frameworks and procedures; squeezing out professional discretion • compliance culture • focus on standardised processes, frameworks and procedures	• variety in responses to meeting need • acceptance of irreducible risk • supportive and enabling management and supervision • learning culture • focus on the service user's needs and beneficial outcomes

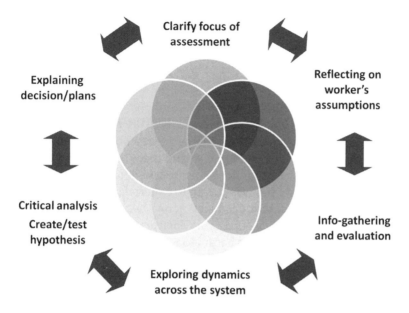

Figure 4.2 Supervision – the six-stage model

The remaining sections of this chapter explore each stage of the cycle and include suggested questions that supervisors may find helpful at each stage. There is inevitable overlap between the stages, and the idea is not to promote yet another rigid framework for conducting assessments, but rather to assist in developing a style of supervision that takes account of the uniqueness and complexity of each situation and enables the social worker to proceed in a way that meets service users' need, operating effectively at the interface of family and professional relationships and organisational expectations.

The six-stage model in practice

Stage 1: Clarifying the focus of the assessment

Fundamental to this stage will be shared understanding of the nature of the assessment task. If the social worker and the supervisor are starting from a different belief about the role and focus of assessment practice, as identified in Table 4.1, the end result is likely to be disagreement about the process and outcome, and the very real possibility that difference will be translated into an apparent performance concern.

Case study

Sarah had recently been on a training course which had promoted the exploration of family history and patterns of behaviour as part of the assessment process. Her supervisor's focus was on the 'here and now': the supervisor felt strongly that it was counterproductive to explore history, and that each problem should be looked at and worked with in relation to current events. This difference in approach was not explored within supervision as time was pressing and there had been no time to discuss the training. Sarah decided to take a full family history for the assessments she was currently undertaking, and as a result missed the deadline for completion on several of them. This was interpreted by the supervisor as poor practice, and the focus of discussion in supervision became Sarah's poor time management.

Even if there is a shared understanding about the fundamental nature of the process it will be important for the supervisor to explore with the social worker the particular issues that might affect *this* particular piece of work.

QUESTIONS FOR SUPERVISION

1. Why have you been asked to carry out this assessment?

2. What is the purpose of the assessment?

3. What questions need to be answered by this assessment?

4. How clear are you about the assessment framework and protocols you should be using? (Rate on a 0–5 scale, where 5 = 'very clear'.)

5. Is the service user aware of the assessment request?

6. How do you plan to involve the service user in the assessment process?

7. How does this assessment fit with other assessments? Where there are other assessments taking place, who is coordinating and has a lead role?

8. Which parts of the assessment process will be more challenging for you?

9. What knowledge base will you need for this assessment?

10. On a scale of 1–10 (10 being 'high'), how confident do you feel about carrying out this assessment?

11. What are the possible outcomes of this type of assessment?

12. What are the limits to this assessment – for example, what can it *not* cover, what risks can't be predicted?

13. What support and guidance do you need from your supervisor?

Stage 2: Reflecting on the supervisee's assumptions

Assumptions will be affected by the social worker's own value base and history, both personal and professional, as well as the context within which he is working. A supervisor who has taken the time to take a supervision history and develop an effective supervision agreement (see Chapter 2) will be much better placed to understand the likely biases the social worker is bringing to the assessment, as well as promoting supervision as being a safe place to explore these without fear of blame. Exploring values, and the prejudices that accompany them, can feel very personal and, for some supervisors, off-limits once a social worker has qualified. Morrison, in his work for the Children's Workforce Development Council (CWDC 2009a), explored the transition from student to newly qualified social worker and identified the importance of considering three aspects of the social worker: their role, identity and self. These are equally important beyond the transition from student to qualified worker, since they are fundamental to who we are and how we respond to service users on a day-to-day basis.

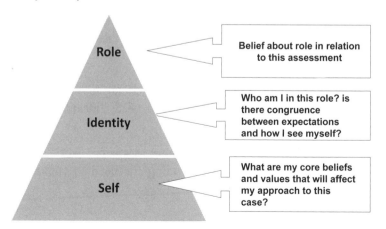

Figure 4.3 Role, identity and self

Case study

Simon was an experienced social worker who had recently joined a disabled children's team after two years working in a referral and assessment team. Simon had found his role in referral and assessment to be fundamentally at odds with how he saw his role as a social worker. The pressure to complete assessments within tight timescales, the limited opportunity to develop quality relationships with service users, did not fit well with his perceived identity as a social worker whose skills lay in relationship-based practice.

Simon was relieved to be working in an environment where he was able to spend more time with families; he had a particular interest in working with disabled children, as his parents had fostered several children with a learning disability and he felt strongly that support for parents could be woefully inadequate.

Simon's first case was that of Jake, aged six, who had multiple impairments. His parents were asking for an increase in short breaks care and the school had expressed some concerns that the parents showed little interest in Jake or his needs. He often came to school in smelly clothes that did not fit, and appeared hungry. Small bruises had been noticed on his legs, which the parents had said were caused by him banging his legs repeatedly against his wheelchair.

In this situation Simon's supervisor will need to consider:

Self:

- How might Simon's personal history affect his approach to the assessment? Is there a possibility that he over-identifies with parents?

- Does Simon operate from the basis of a social model of disability or does he see the child as the problem?

Identity:

- How does Simon see his role vis-à-vis (a) supporting the parents while (b) ensuring that Jake's needs (including need for protection) are assessed?

- How far does Simon see his identity as a social worker in a disabled children's team as including the need to challenge parents where appropriate?

Role:

- Is Simon clear that his role as a social worker in this team includes child protection work?

Values will affect our intuitive responses and, in the example above, if Simon's value base stems from a belief that that disabled people are a burden and their carers need sympathy, he will be less likely to explore any possibility that Jake might be suffering harm.

Munro (2008) explores how our conscious thinking is influenced by our intuitive responses to a far greater extent than was previously understood. In the light of this supervisors need to recognise the richness of the information that intuitive responses bring to the table. The 'gut reaction' is something to be valued within supervision, and exploration of the social worker's initial responses and assumptions will help the supervisor to identify areas within the case that need further exploration, as well as indicating where individual bias may be skewing practice. Exploration of Simon's gut reaction to the referral may reveal that his immediate thought is that more short break care is needed immediately, in order to relieve the stress on the parents. The good supervisor will explore the origins of this reaction and help to ensure that the assessment gathers all the necessary information for a reasoned judgement to be reached.

Supervisors should expect social workers to be biased, and work with these biases, using an understanding of the impact they may have on reasoning. Munro (2008) makes the point that we should aim to detect and minimise bias by using conscious and analytical reasoning, taking account of the psychological processes that are likely to impact on practice. At the early stage of the assessment process social workers are likely to cling to their beliefs about a given situation, and when faced with evidence that challenges their point of view they are likely to:

- avoid focusing on that aspect of the assessment
- forget information that does not fit their preconceived ideas
- reject information that is contrary to their beliefs
- reinterpret evidence to fit their own point of view.

By exploring assumptions early on in the process, before the social worker embarks upon extensive information gathering, the supervisor has the opportunity to identify those initial beliefs and assumptions which the social worker may tend to hold onto as the assessment progresses, even though emerging evidence indicates an alternative viewpoint.

Supervisors therefore need to be acutely aware of the factors that might be affecting the assessment process from an early stage, and to work with the supervisee to identify them. One tool that has been found useful for both practitioners and supervisors is the 'cultural review' developed by McCracken (1988). This can be used either by the individual practitioner or as the basis for a joint exploration within supervision.

SUPERVISION TOOL – THE CULTURAL REVIEW
(Adapted from McCracken 1988)

Work with the supervisee to help her explore:

1. What do I know about service users in this situation?

2. Where does my knowledge come from?

3. What prejudices might I bring?

4. What do I expect about families/individuals in this situation?

5. What might surprise me about this situation and why would it be a surprise?

6. How might the service users in this situation perceive me?

7. How might my organisation be perceived?

8. What impact might this assessment have on the service users and their families in this situation?

9. What agency norms and practices will influence my assessment (e.g. thresholds, practice standards/expectations?

REFLECTION – QUESTIONS FOR SUPERVISION

1. List three assumptions you might have formed on the basis of the information you already have about this case.

2. What previous experience do you have of assessment work in similar cases?

3. How do you think that might influence your approach?

4. What was the outcome last time you worked with a similar situation?

5. Does this situation remind you of any similar situations, either at work or elsewhere?

6. If you had any bias in this case, what would it be?

7. What beliefs do other professionals already have about this family/person?

8. What issues might arise in this assessment in relation to race, culture, language, gender, disability or sexual orientation?

9. How might the service user feel about you?

10. What might his feelings be about this particular assessment?

11. What information does the user need in order to give informed consent to the assessment?

12. What do you think will be the most challenging aspects of the assessment for the service user?

Stage 3: Information gathering and evaluation

It is often said that social workers are good at gathering information but less good at analysing it. Frameworks used for assessment are likely to specify the information required, and one task for the supervisor will be to assist the social worker in considering how to obtain and document the relevant information. However, there is a danger that frameworks may lull social workers and their supervisors into a false sense of security in the belief that they know all there is to know. A careful consideration of assessment practice is likely to reveal that, regardless of any frameworks, information is gathered according to the bias of the worker, and will be affected by the quality of relationships with service users and professionals across the network. Information is too often gathered without being evaluated for quality or relevance, and there is little consideration of the all-important question 'What don't we know?'

According to Morrison, 'Raw information is almost always complex and problematic. However, good supervision can help to test and explore assumptions, ambiguities or gaps in information, ensuring that analysis and planning are on solid foundations' (CWDC 2009a).

Morrison uses the idea of interrogating discrepancy in order to evaluate information, and identifies five types of discrepancy that supervisors should be alert to when supervising any assessment process.

FIVE TYPES OF DISCREPANCY

1. *Informational*: there is contradictory information from various sources.

2. *Interpretative*: different conclusions are drawn from the same information by different professionals.

3. *Interactive*: the service user's declared intentions are contradicted by actions.

4. *Incongruent*: the service user talks about her situation in an inconsistent, contradictory or incoherent manner.

5. *Instinctual*: the worker's gut feelings suggest that something is wrong, but he cannot specify what.

The presence of discrepancies should trigger further exploration as to their origin, relevance, and impact on the judgements and decisions made. The following adapted version of Morrison's discrepancy matrix has been used with supervisors to assist them initially in naming discrepancies, and from there in working with supervisees to decide what needs to happen next.

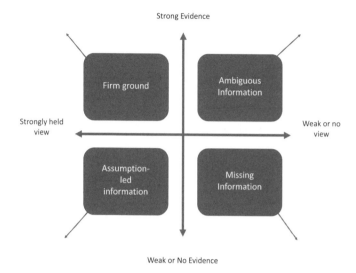

Figure 4.4 The discrepancy matrix

Information in each of the four quadrants will need to be scrutinised and tested in order either to move it into (or retain it on) firm ground, or to eliminate it as irrelevant or ungrounded.

QUESTIONS FOR SUPERVISION

1. What are the key pieces of information required in this assessment?

2. What do we already know?

3. What don't we know?

4. Where and who are the agency sources for this information?

5. Who knows the family/person best?

6. How might other agencies see your role in this situation?

7. Is any agency likely to be difficult to engage? How might we address this?

8. Would there be any benefit in undertaking some/all of the assessment on a co-worker basis or a multidisciplinary basis?

9. Which family members and friends need to be involved, and in what order or grouping?

10. How will the information be recorded?

11. How will you evaluate the quality of the information received from other agencies?

12. What discrepancies in information exist?

13. How do we test or resolve these?

Stage 4: Exploring dynamics across the system

At this point the supervisee will be working with increasingly complex information which will include intuitive responses to face-to-face contact with service users, their families and other professionals in the system. Supervision therefore needs to move beyond the checklist approach of ensuring that tasks have been carried out and forms filled in, to engaging with the social worker in an exploration of the dynamics of relationships. This will include family relationships, the relationship between the social worker and service user, and relationships within the professional network. Alongside this the supervisor will need to consider how her own relationship with the supervisee may be affecting practice, drawing on her knowledge of the impact of supervisory style on outcomes, as explored in Chapter 3.

Many social work assessments will be exploring complex family relationships, and supervisors need to be able to grasp these quickly. Genograms, as a tool for social work with families, have been in use for many years and are an invaluable visual tool for supervisors to use to gain a quick, in-depth understanding of key aspects of family dynamics, and to identify what missing information might assist the assessment process. Often, information about key family members is missing from assessment reports, and there is a lost opportunity to explore the impact of the past on the present. Understanding the dynamics of family relationships can assist not only the assessment but also the intervention, and understanding of the way in which various family members are responding within the context of the social work relationship.

SUPERVISION TOOL – USING GENOGRAMS TO EXPLORE FAMILY RELATIONSHIPS

Genograms:

- enable supervisors to assimilate complex information about the family

- assist prompt identification of missing information

- provide the opportunity for the supervisor to ask the worker what patterns of protective and risk factors are present in the current family situation, and in particular how these have been forged or changed across generations

- create the opportunity for supervisors to ask workers how they engaged family members in reflecting on the impact of family history on their confidence and capacity to parent

- enable supervisors and practitioners to work together exploring challenges or blocks in the social worker's relationship with family members; in particular identifying whether this relationship is mirroring any concerning or dangerous dynamics within the family system.

When using genograms in supervision:

- Compile them together rather than simply reviewing one already on file. The process of working together will emphasise the collaborative nature of supervision and help you to understand how the social worker is feeling and thinking about the family.

- Remember that a genogram is far more than 'who is who' and 'who was who'. It's about the meaning of family members and their behaviours to each other, and in particular how this positions the expectations of, and care available to, the child.

- Pay attention to the genogram's emotional impact on the supervisee. Unanticipated reactions may arise where family patterns and relationships 'push buttons' for the social worker.

(Adapted from CWDC 2009b.)

One area that may need particular attention at this stage is the relationship between the social worker and a service user who is apparently resistant to social work intervention. There will also be a particular issue where there are possible safeguarding concerns for children or adults.

SUPERVISION AND 'RESISTANT' SERVICE USERS

Social workers are working on a day-to-day basis with families who are experiencing crises and/or varying degrees of trauma and who may not always welcome social work help. Negotiating these relationships whilst remaining focused on the primary reason for social work intervention requires skill, emotional intelligence and the capacity for managing complex emotions – emotions which will affect the worker as well as the family.

The issue of social work with 'resistant' families has come to the fore particularly as a result of serious case reviews into situations where children have died or been seriously injured. Workers across the professions in both children's and adults' services have been found to be overly optimistic, reluctant to challenge, and at times deflected by families who appeared to be cooperating but in fact were not doing so. However, the term 'resistance' needs to be used with caution, as it can appear to locate the problem solely with the service user, rather than considering the many factors which may be contributing to reluctance to accept social work intervention. These factors may reside just as easily in the capacity of the organisation or individual social worker to work in a way that makes sense to service users as in the service users themselves, and the exploration of 'resistance' may give the supervisor an ideal opportunity to assess the skills of the social worker in forming and working effectively with relationships. For supervisors, the challenge is to provide a safe place where supervisees can explore the possible meaning of a service user's response to social work help, the emotional impact of this response, and the impact their own interventions may be having on the dynamics of a case. Supervision will therefore need to take a holistic approach to understanding the many contributory factors which may be involved in the apparently resistant behaviour.

As shown in Figure 4.5, the supervisor will need to focus on:

1. what the social worker is bringing to the interaction

2. the content and quality of the social work intervention

3. the possible impact of social work intervention on the service user

4. the social worker's response to the service user.

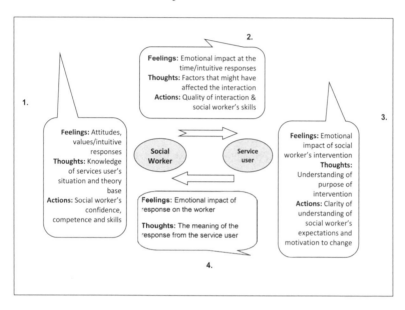

Figure 4.5 Interaction between social worker and service user

A knowledge review focusing on 51 key pieces of evidence from 2000 to 2009 (Fauth *et al.* 2010) provides a comprehensive account of the research in relation to 'resistance' as it relates to children's safeguarding, and is a useful resource for supervisors. A theme throughout the studies is one of social workers being perceived by parents as lacking basic interpersonal skills, coming across as uncaring, judgemental and not listening to the parents' point of view. The studies deliver a consistent message about the importance of effective supervision. For example, a study by Gardner (2008) noted that when practitioners felt overwhelmed, their confidence was low, or they were not receiving adequate managerial support, they tended to avoid making difficult decisions or challenging their colleagues' decisions and behaviours, even when they had reason to believe that a child was at serious risk of suffering harm. However, although the research into 'resistance' indicates the importance of supervision, the review notes that there is little evidence within the studies as to what the key components of good supervision are.

One important study by Forrester *et al.* (2008) explored the way in which social workers talk to families about child welfare concerns. The research moved beyond retrospective accounts of practice to using vignettes to identify how social workers are likely to respond in particular situations. They describe the most striking finding as the high level of confrontation and low level of listening shown by social workers. Empathy did not reach the level generally accepted to be the basic level for helpful interaction, and responses are described by the researchers as actually diminishing the possibility of meaningful partnership working between practitioner and parents. The fact that these results were so consistent across the whole research sample suggests that these problems in the social worker/family interaction are a systemic issue, rather than a result of individual poor practice. As a result the researchers call for more guidance and training in respect of the micro-skills needed for successful social work. Guidance and training will, however, need to be translated into day-to-day practice and backed up by supervisors who are interested in exploring the skill set of their supervisees and examining what actually happened in the interaction between worker and service user. Supervision which focuses solely on outputs and tasks will not get to the heart of the exchange between worker and family. Supervisors need to be attuned to the myriad factors that might be influencing the interaction, and to work with the social worker to understand these and consider implications for future practice.

Working with 'resistance' is a complex task, and supervisors need to be aware of social work skills that might be more likely to facilitate change. A study in England carried out for the Office of the Children's Commissioner (Wiffin 2010) involved speaking both to social workers and to families who had been defined as 'resistant'. Although this study focused on families where there were child welfare concerns, it is likely that the messages are relevant in any situation where social workers are working with families who may not welcome their intervention. The study found that social workers who were most likely to facilitate positive engagement were those who:

- demonstrated respect
- understood the barriers, including fears about having a social worker
- worked in partnership
- showed that they cared
- communicated openly and honestly
- had knowledge, expertise and access to resources
- had the skill and capacity to develop relationships.

Supervisors need to find ways to understand the skills that social workers are using in their day-to-day practice. Ways of achieving this might be:

1. direct observation of practice
2. co-working
3. role play in supervision
4. service user feedback.

Points to consider

1. When was the last time you observed one of your supervisees practise?
2. What did this tell you about her skills in:
   - ✓ showing empathy
   - ✓ demonstrating respect
   - ✓ communicating clearly, openly and honestly
   - ✓ challenging where necessary?
3. If you haven't observed practice recently – how can you plan to do so?

Working with individual performance is further explored in Chapter 5.

SUPERVISION, COMMUNICATION AND PROFESSIONAL RELATIONSHIPS

Another key aspect of dynamics that needs to be explored at this stage of the cycle relates to the social worker's relationships with other professionals in the network.

Social workers work at the interface of many organisations and professional relationships. At times these are relatively easy to navigate, and at other times the challenges may seem immense. At the core of the way organisations and individuals relate to each other is communication, and the way communication patterns play out and are understood by those involved can have a profound effect on the quality of assessments and interventions with service users. A key role for any social work supervisor is therefore to work with the supervisee to understand the meaning and impact of communication across the network.

Reder and Duncan (2003) emphasise the importance of understanding the psychology of communication between professionals. They define communication as *the process by which information is transferred from one person to another and is understood by them,* and emphasise that when one person transfers a message to another, a process of meta-communication (communication about the communication) takes place. This relates to the way in which nonverbal components such as tone and emotional content either reinforce the message or qualify it. Information therefore includes feelings, attitudes, beliefs and desires, as well as factual information. For example, a simple communication such as 'I suggest you do not do that' could mean either 'Please consider whether you wish to do that', or 'On no account do that!' depending on the tone of voice.

Too often we concentrate on the content of communication and do not explore whether the giver and the recipient have a shared understanding of its meaning. It is the responsibility of both the message giver and the receiver to ensure that each understands the communication, thereby monitoring mutual understanding.

Case study

A referral has been received by Children's Social Care concerning a five-year-old girl who is regularly arriving at school saying she has not had any breakfast. Her clothes smell to the extent that other children will not sit with her, and today her teacher has noticed a large bruise on the side of her head for which she can give no explanation. The family are not known to local health visitors or school nurses, as they only moved to the area within the last 12 months.

As part of the enquiries the social worker telephoned the family's GP and asked, 'Do you have any child protection concerns about this child?' The GP replied, 'No.' Later the supervisor asked whether the social worker had contacted the GP and was told that there had been no risks identified that would indicate child protection concerns.

In fact, the GP is aware that the father has a long-standing alcohol problem and has been treated for depression. However, the GP did not interpret the question, 'Do you have child protection concerns about this child?' as related to parental alcohol and mental health issues, since a large number of patients with such issues cared very well for their children. The social worker assumed that any information might be associated with a contributory risk factor would be shared.

The supervisor could have asked:

- What do you think the GP thought your question meant?

- Did you check that the GP understood the type of information that might constitute 'child protection concerns'?

- Have you had previous contact with this GP? – How might that have affected his response to you?

Supervision can provide an important forum for the social worker to reflect on any 'below the surface' communication that may be taking place. This might be caused by feelings about another person or organisation, anxieties and workload pressures, or personal beliefs and prejudices. Supervision must move beyond an approach which ensures simply that communication happened, to collaborating with the supervisee in interrogating the meaning of the communication, and hence its effectiveness.

THE MEANING OF COMMUNICATION: WHAT DO SUPERVISORS NEED TO DO?

1. *Acknowledge that communication occurred*
   'Did you telephone the doctor?'
   'So we received another referral from the housing association about Mrs Sanders.'

2. *Explore the detail of the communication*
   'What did you ask? What was their response?'
   'How was the referral made? What were the concerns this time?'

3. *Explore feelings and emotions within the communication*
   'What happened when you last spoke to them and how did you feel about it?'
   'What do you believe they feel about you?'
   'How do you feel about the information/response?'

4. *Understand the meaning of the communication*
   'How far has the quality or content of the communication between you been affected by previous experiences or current expectations?'
   'How might they perceive your role – what are their expectations of you? Are there any issues of power and hierarchy that may have affected the communication?'

5. *Explore the implications of the communication*
   'Do we need to ask any further questions?'
   'What needs to happen next?'

COMMUNICATION WITHIN GROUPS – UNDERSTANDING 'GROUPTHINK'

As social workers will often be working with groups, both within and across professional boundaries, and many crucial judgements and decisions are made within a group context, time is needed in supervision to explore the way group processes are influencing decision making.

A psychologist, Janis (1982), coined the term 'groupthink' to explain findings of research studies which clearly identified the distorted reasoning that can result from biases within groups. Groupthink is described by Janis as a drive for consensus without the realistic consideration of alternative ideas, and 'A mode of thinking that people engage in when they are deeply involved in a cohesive in-group, when members' striving for unanimity overrides their motivation to realistically appraise alternative courses of action' (Janis 1982, p.120).

Characteristics of groupthink include:

- an overestimation of the group, creating an illusion of invulnerability and unquestioned belief in the group's inherent morality

- closed-mindedness, resulting in collective efforts to discount alternative ideas, and the perpetuation of stereotyped views of outsiders

- pressures towards conformity directed towards any group member who dissents from the majority view.

Within child care, research into the functioning of child protection conferences (Prince *et al.* 2005) identified groupthink in action, with clear evidence of little visible dissent and the views of a small, powerful group dominating. Anecdotal evidence also suggests that for many people who do not view themselves as 'experts', attending conferences is a daunting process and they feel unable to challenge the views of those who they believe to have more knowledge and expertise than themselves. The disturbing feature of this situation is that it may be those who feel unable to voice their views who have more day-to-day contact with the child. This has many features of the 'exaggeration of hierarchy' described by Reder and Duncan (1993), whereby those are perceived to be higher up the professional hierarchy are listened to more than those who have a more lowly status, even though they know the family the best.

If one important role of supervision is to promote critical thinking, paying attention to the functioning of groups is an important aspect of the supervisory process, since evidence suggests that the strong tendency for groups to avoid conflict acts against critical thinking (Munro 2008) and it is also an obstacle to lead making the best decisions, since 'the tendency for groups to reach consensus does not lead to middle-of-the-road decisions, but to "extreme" ones; that is, the group will shift to one extreme or the other, either being very cautious or very risky' (Munro 2008, p.148–149).

Janis proposed measures to avoid groupthink, which include group members discussing the group's deliberations with trusted associates, and Prince *et al.* recommend that there should be opportunities to discuss group processes outside the group. Supervision for social workers can fulfil this role.

EXPLORING GROUPTHINK – QUESTIONS FOR SUPERVISION

1. How did you feel about the outcome of the meeting?
   - comfortable?
   - perturbed?
   - surprised?
2. Who took the lead during the meeting?
3. Who spoke most?
4. Did anyone remain silent throughout?
5. Were there disagreements and challenges to each others' points of view?
6. Did you feel your point of view was heard and respected?
7. Did you disagree with anyone and challenge them during the meeting?
8. Was there any point where you decided not to challenge another's point of view? If so, what was the reason for this?

SUPERVISION TOOL – USING ECOMAPS TO REFLECT ON THE DYNAMICS OF THE PROFESSIONAL NETWORK

Ecomaps have been used for some time as a tool for working with families to explore relationships between family members and others within their immediate network. An ecomap is a graphical representation that shows all of the systems at play in an individual's life (for an explanation and illustration see Wilson *et al.* 2008, p.298.) They can equally be a useful tool for supervisors working with supervisees to explore and understand, quickly and visually, the nature of relationships across complex professional networks.

Figure 4.6 is an ecomap representing the professional network surrounding 'Nina'.

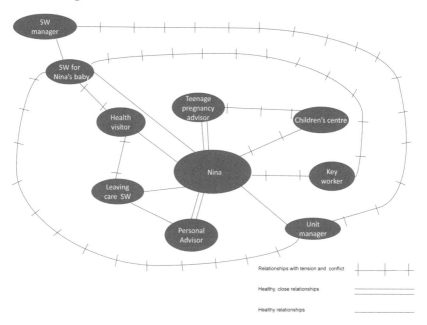

Figure 4.6 Ecomap for Nina

Case study

Nina is an 18-year-old parent living with her baby in a semi-independent unit with staff support from 9am to 5pm each day. Previously a young person in foster care, she moved to this accommodation as part of the leaving care arrangement, and this forms part of a new strategy in the children's services to use this provision and carry out community assessments, as opposed to using residential 'mother and baby' units. This is a significant change for social workers, as they now are required to coordinate the assessments across the professional network and manage their anxieties about increased risks.

What might this ecomap tell the supervisor and her supervisee?

1. There are tensions between the social worker and some of the key professionals in the network around Nina, which are likely to be jeopardising the services she and her baby are receiving.

2. There are a number of healthy, close relationships within the network that need to be maintained.

3. There is a split between the professionals working with Nina and those involved to work with her baby.

4. The supervisee needs support to manage her role, which might require some direct involvement of the supervisor.

REFLECTION – QUESTIONS FOR SUPERVISION

1. How would you describe your approach to assessment?

2. What would I notice about it?

3. How do you think (the service user) would describe your approach and style? If you had to describe the dynamics between you and the family/individual, would it be more like 'cat and mouse', 'pulling teeth', 'a shared voyage of discovery', 'just another assessment' – or something else?

4. Who or what does this assessment remind you of?

5. What is your gut reaction about this family/individual? Where does this come from?

6. What is easy/hard to talk about in this assessment?

7. What has most surprised/concerned you about this family/person?

8. What, if any, contradictory or confusing signals have you picked up in the interaction between the service user/family members and yourself and/or other professionals?

9. Which family members are harder to reach in this assessment?

10. What have you noticed in relation to the professional network in relation to

- ◦ cohesion vs conflict
- ◦ subordination vs domination
- ◦ who is 'in' and who is 'out'
- ◦ whose voices are not heard?

11. To what extent does your experience of the situation mirror the experience of individuals within it? What might this tell you about what is going on in this situation?

Stage 5: Critical analysis

At this stage of the process, particularly in complex cases, the supervisor and social worker are likely to have a sense of drowning in information. Serious case reviews in children's services have all too often found that professionals working with children and adults feel overwhelmed by overwhelming families with the result that focus is lost and action is not taken to protect the child. Although 'critical analysis' may sound as if it is a cognitive process, in fact the capacity of the supervisor to work with emotions positively at this stage may make all the difference between an analysis that leads to appropriate action and one that does not.

Case study

The police have had several calls from Neville, a 79-year-old man who originates from Grenada. He calls to report violence from his grandson, but when the police attend the home he sends them away and retracts his allegations. Neville appears to have been drinking heavily on these occasions. The grandson is well known to the police and has a history of drug and theft offences. Neville and his wife (now deceased) raised their grandson and Neville promised his wife that he would always take care of him. Recently Neville's health has deteriorated and he has had a number of minor strokes. A safeguarding adults investigation has started and a social worker has been allocated. Whilst Neville has spoken about giving his grandson significant amounts of money, he tends to minimise any problems in their relationship. Neville presents as a confident man, who is always meticulously dressed and prides himself on his appearance.

Although on one level the surface information could lead to case closure, as Neville does not want to make a complaint, it is important for the supervisor to allow the social worker to explore his intuitive responses and biases relating to both Neville and his grandson, and to begin to formulate hypotheses about what might really be happening in this situation.

The tasks for the supervisor at this stage are therefore to work with the supervisee to integrate the intuitive and evidence-based information and use it to formulate ideas about what it might mean. The supervisor will need to:

1. assess and develop the social worker's capacity for critical thought

2. develop hypotheses with the social worker about what might be happening in the case, based on intuition and evidence-based knowledge (a hypothesis is a testable statement such as 'Neville is suffering from short-term memory loss')

3. test the hypotheses against the information, and identify whether further work needs to be done in order to test them more fully

4. refer to the questions that were to be answered by the assessment, and check whether these have been addressed by the assessment process so far.

Social work frequently involves forming judgements about situations where there are no definitive answers. Critical thinking and analysis in social work therefore involves the social worker in holding on to uncertainty and constantly re-evaluating information. The supervisor will therefore be developing the supervisee's capacity to contextualise, evaluate and compare evidence in order to reach a decision that no one can yet be certain is the 'right' decision.

Critical thinking and analysis in social work is therefore not simply an intellectual activity; the capacity for critical thought also has a direct impact on, and is affected by, the capacity of workers for empathy and self-awareness. Holtz Deal 2004 note that: 'Studies have shown that trainees with higher levels of critical thinking skills are more empathetic and self aware…empathic skills are both cognitive and relational' (Holtz Deal 2004, p.43).

King and Kitchener developed a model (adapted in Table 4.2) to describe the process of developing critical thought, and although this is described as a linear model, supervisors need to be mindful that social workers will move back and forth between stages, depending on the context. For example, the very experienced social worker who has been displaying a high level of critical thinking is likely to retreat to Stage 2 when feeling under threat. Once again, the need to be aware of current stressors and the emotional response to the work is crucial at this stage.

Table 4.2 Critical thinking and reflective judgement (adapted from King and Kitchener 1994)

Stage	Example
1. Knowledge and beliefs are assumed to be absolute and concrete.	'I know my assessment is right.'
2. Knowledge is certain but not always immediately available.	'When we have a new procedure we will be able to make the right decision.'
3. We may have the answers in the future.	'A new procedure may not help, so I will rely on my own beliefs and opinions.'
4. Knowledge is acknowledged to be uncertain but idiosyncratic arguments and evidence are used to justify beliefs.	'Noone else has the answers, so my explanation is as good as anybody's.'
5. Knowledge needs to be put in context and is affected by perceptions.	'I was trained to use solution-focused approaches, others in my team use psychodynamic approaches – what works best depends on how you understand human nature.'
6. Compares and evaluates evidence across contexts.	'I will decide which approach to use by comparing which approaches have been found to work best in these circumstances.'
7. Knowledge is constantly evaluated against new evidence.	'Weighing up the knowledge about what works, along with my own past experiences and beliefs, I have developed an action plan.'

The supervisor's task in developing the capacity for critical thought is therefore to recognise when external factors may adversely affect the supervisee's capacity for critical thought, and prevent slippage from higher to lower levels.

Key supervision activities might be:

- reviewing the social worker's workload to provide challenging experiences

- recognising the demands of new experiences and putting in place the necessary supports (e.g. co-working, mentoring)

- reflecting on the knowledge-base needed to work with the demands of their caseload

- reflecting on the supervisor's own knowledge-base and capacity for providing the level of knowledge and expertise required

- planning how to fill knowledge gaps for both supervisor and the supervisee.

QUESTIONS FOR SUPERVISION

1. What is becoming clearer? What is becoming less clear? What is unknown?

2. What positive or concerning patterns are emerging?

3. How long-standing are these patterns?

4. To what extent does the information gathered confirm or challenge your initial impressions?

5. What pieces of information are still not making sense or are ambiguous?

6. How can ambiguous information be clarified?

7. How do other agencies understand the situation?

8. What is the user's explanation for the situation she is in?

9. What might other professionals or service users make of how we are thinking about this assessment and its implications?

10. How can we test which explanation is likely to be more robust?

11. What knowledge, theory, research, values and experience can help explain this situation and how it might develop?

12. What specific outcomes do we need to be seeing in order to address the issues identified?

13. If there is no professional intervention, will things be better, worse or the same in six months' time?

Stage 6: Explaining decision and plans

Social workers need to be able to defend the decisions they make and able to explain the reasons for the plans that are being put in place. Effective supervision will interrogate the thinking behind decisions and plans, and by doing so will make sure that the social worker is on firm ground when explaining these in other areas, such as in care planning meetings, case conferences, professionals' meetings and court. To a large extent it is this stage that will test the effectiveness of the whole assessment process and the extent to which supervision has facilitated clarity of thought and judgement. Wilson *et al.* (2008) note that:

> Endings always relate to beginnings – they are influenced by them and are influences on them. If a clear remit for the assessment process has been identified at the outset it enhances the likelihood of a more effective and accurate outcome being reached… It is hoped that if this cyclical and reflexive behaviour has permeated the assessment process then the recommended course of action should come as no surprise and should have evolved out of the discussions that have taken place. (p.292)

SUPERVISION TOOL TO ASSIST DECISION MAKING – DECISION TREES

Decision trees are particularly useful as a supervision tool when:

- the social worker and supervisor have arrived at a different conclusion regarding the course of action that needs to be taken

- both are unclear about the best way forward or how to explain the rationale for their decision-making to others.

Detailed accounts of the use of decision trees are given in Munro (2002, 2008) and Dalzell and Sawyer (2007).

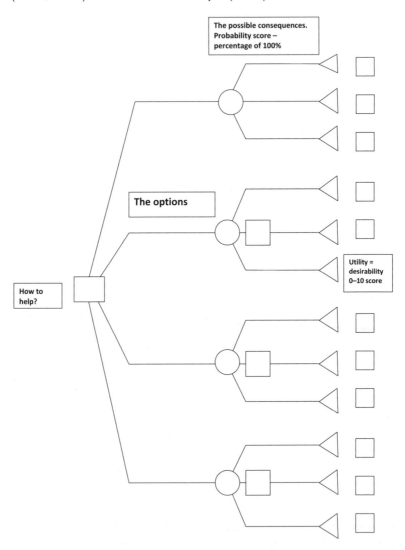

Figure 4.7 Decision tree

Using the outline tree (Figure 4.7), the process within supervision would be:

1. Identify the decision that has to be made – for example, should we recommend care proceedings?

2. What are the possible choices (up to four *options*)? Write these on the lines emerging from the square – for example, care proceedings and removal; care proceedings and child remains at home; further child protection plan; remove from child protection plan.

3. What are the possible *consequences* of each option? Write these along the lines emerging from the four circles – for example, for 'care proceedings and remain at home', the consequences might be: further abuse; abuse stops and compliant behaviour; relationship between social worker and parents breaks down; increased motivation to change.

4. Give a *probability* score to each consequence, where 0 per cent = 'will not happen' and 100 per cent = 'definitely will happen'. The total score across all consequences should be 100 per cent.

5. Using professional judgement, decide on the *desirability* of each consequence and ascribe a score from 0 to 10 where 0 = 'least desirable' and 10 = 'totally desirable'.

6. For each consequence, multiply the *probability* score by the *desirability* score and then add together the results for all of the consequences of the relevant option. Write this overall score in the square for the relevant option. The option with the highest overall score is the one that combines the most realistic chance of success with the highest desirability.

It may be useful for the supervisor and social worker to complete separate decision trees and then come together to compare their findings. This approach is particularly productive when moving on from a polarised position where there are competing points of view, as it helps to identify those points which are the most crucial or difficult for that particular decision. Although some people may find the mathematical aspects of this tool at odds with the other approaches to supervision outlined in this guide, it's important to try to stick with it. Ascribing numerical values forces people to 'nail their colours to the mast' and provides a focus for exploring the detail of the decision making process.

EXPLAINING DECISIONS AND PLANS – QUESTIONS FOR SUPERVISION

1. What decisions do we need to make at this point?

2. What options are there?

3. To what extent do we have the information to make a decision at this point?

4. What might be the pros and cons of different decisions? Who gains and who loses?

5. What is negotiable and non-negotiable about this situation in relation to our organisation's duties and responsibilities?

6. What evidence exists about the willingness and ability of the user to understand, engage with and address the issues identified?

7. To what extent is there agreement between organisations about the main issues and how each organisation will contribute to addressing these?

8. What efforts have already been made to address the issues in this case? What has worked? How can we build on this?

9. What specific outcomes have been or need to be identified in the intervention plan?

10. To what extent would these outcomes make sense to the service user in the light of the analysis and the assessment process?

11. How clear are your/others' roles and specific tasks in helping these outcomes become a reality?

12. How does the plan provide for monitoring and review against the intended outcomes?

13. What is the contingency plan if these aren't achieved?

14. How clear are you about the framework for writing up this assessment/assessment report?

Supervision and the management of risk

All assessments will to a greater or lesser extent involve consideration of risk at all stages. However, at the point where decision and plans are being formulated, it may be necessary to address explicitly how risks are to be managed, and risk assessment throughout the process should already have involved:

- assessing the likelihood of harm and of benefit

- systematically gathering information about past and present concerns

- analysing the information to determine both the likelihood and potential seriousness of any risk of harm

- identifying the presence and significance of protective factors

- coming to an overall judgement about the level of risk.

Where risks have been identified, managing risk will involve the identification of:

1. the factors which may lead to risks occurring

2. the undesirable impact of any risk

3. how best to increase potential benefits.

(Titterton 2005)

Using the six-stage model for the management of risk

Following the six-stage model, critical questions for supervisors in relation to the assessment and management of risk include:

1. What risk factors have been identified in this case?

2. What is the worker's knowledge base about risk assessment and management in relation to the issues in this case?

3. What is the quality of multidisciplinary working and how does this help or hinder the worker's capacity to manage risk?

4. What are the protective factors in this case? How can they be enhanced?

5. In terms of managing risk, how will the assessment be explained, communicated and evidenced to family and professionals?

6. How effective is the social worker in engaging family members and other professionals in constructing and maintaining a viable risk management plan?

7. How clear are the worker, family members and other professionals about the review process and the consequences and contingencies, should the plan fail?

8. How confident and competent is the worker to carry out his responsibilities and tasks under the risk management plan?

9. What critical support and oversight does the supervisor need to supply?

(Adapted from Morrison and Wonnacott 2009.)

Conclusion

Assessment is an essential aspect of the social work role and involves complex use of skills and knowledge. Supervision of assessment needs to address the different levels of practice; these range from the practical level through to the psychological and analytical. Supervisors need to work at all levels. The six-stage model developed by Tony Morrison (Morrison and Wonnacott 2009) provides a framework to support this. Really effective supervision will move beyond dialogue, to the supervisor working actively with the supervisee to understand all aspects of the case and reach a position where the supervisee is able to articulate clearly the reasons behind her decisions.

Issues from this chapter to discuss with your supervisor

1. How might the six-stage model for the supervision of assessment practice apply in my setting?

2. Which of the following tools might be most useful in this team?

✓ genograms?

✓ ecomaps?

✓ discrepancy matrix?

✓ decision trees.?

3. How well do I currently know the quality of the interaction between my supervisees and service users? What steps can I take to improve this?

4. How defensible is the decision making of my supervisees? Can we currently explain clearly to others the basis of decisions and plans? How can this be improved though supervision?

Further reading and resources

Dalzell, R. and Sawyer, E. (2007) *Putting Analysis into Assessment*. London: National Children's Bureau.

Gast, L. and Patmore, A. (2012) *Mastering Approaches to Diversity in Social Work*. London: Jessica Kingsley Publishers. Chapter 6.

Holland, S. (2004) *Child and Family Assessment in Social Work Practice*. London: Sage.

Titterton, M. (2005) *Risk and Risk Taking in Health and Social Welfare*. London: Jessica Kingsley Publishers.

Wilson, K., Ruch, G., Lymbery, M. and Cooper, A. (2008) *Social Work, an Introduction to Contemporary Practice*. Harlow: Pearson. NB p.287: a case study linking construction of the genogram to the development of relationship-based approaches to work with a family.

Note: Although many of these resources have originated in children's services, they have been tested working with supervisors in adults' services and have been found to be just as effective in that setting.

CHAPTER 5

Understanding and Managing Individual Performance

Key messages from this chapter

- Recognising good practice is a fundamental part of continuous improvement.

- Balancing support and challenge is key to good supervision.

- Early recognition and attention to performance concerns is crucial.

- The causes of poor performance need to be understood in order to develop effective solutions.

- The 'bottom line' must be ensuring delivery of the best possible service to the service user.

It emerges from training courses with social work supervisors that one of the most concerning aspects of their work is dealing with situations where they are worried about the performance of one of their supervisees. They are acutely aware of the consequences of poor practice for service users, the organisation and the reputation of the profession, yet often report feeling ill-equipped to balance the need both to challenge poor practice and to provide the right intervention to support service improvements. A variety of concerns can be at the heart of these dilemmas:

- challenging the practice of supervisees who were formally peers (where a supervisor has been promoted from within the team)

- unravelling the relative impact on performance of workload pressures, organisational tensions (such a restructuring), knowledge and skill deficits, personal issues and lack of resources to do the job well

- being accused of unfairness/racism/sexism/disablism, etc.

- knowing what to do to make a positive difference

- lack of clarity about Human Resources (HR) process and feeling unsure about the support they will receive if they feel there is a need to use formal procedures.

Points to consider

- Faced with a worry about the performance of one of your supervisees, would any of the above bulleted points be true for you?

- How has this influenced your approach to addressing individual performance issues?

- Are there any other factors that you can think of that might concern you about managing performance concerns?

This chapter is focused on taking a positive approach to managing individual performance within supervision, and on seeing working with performance issues as intricately bound up with practice development. This is yet another example of where integration of supervision functions occurs, with management and staff development functions both coming to the fore. The approach taken here is that part of the supervisory role is to assess the quality of practice, and to work with supervisees and the organisation to improve quality continuously by developing staff. This takes place at the same time as spotting and responding to performance concerns. The starting point is therefore the role of the supervisor as a practice leader who ensures that the supervisory process enables supervisees to:

- reflect critically on their performance

- find innovative solutions to practice dilemmas

- identify learning and development needs.

Where necessary within this framework, the supervisor will be able to spot concerns about performance, understand what is causing these and respond accordingly.

Management of practice and staff development go hand-in-hand, and supervision is the forum where the two meet. Managing individual performance is therefore on a continuum from staff development through performance concerns to HR intervention, with the core principle being all the way that every service user must receive the highest possible standard of social work practice. This will also ultimately result in the added bonus of improved public confidence and a stronger profession.

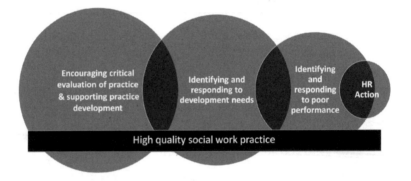

Figure 5.1 The performance improvement continuum

As the supervisor and supervisee work together in supervision to reflect critically on practice, the role of the supervisor will be to support the social worker in considering how he can develop his practice knowledge and skills in line with the requirements of his role. This should also involve stretching the social worker and encouraging innovation and the development of new ideas. In doing so it is likely that development needs will be identified, and part of the supervisory process will involve planning together how these needs can be met. In a smaller number of instances this process will uncover performance concerns which will require a response; in a minority of situations these will not be amenable to intervention, and in order to protect service users HR action will be needed. It is this bottom line of the rights of all service users to high quality social work practice that must be assured throughout the whole process.

This will, of course, link with other management processes, such as appraisal systems, with a continuous flow of information between the two. At the point of formal annual appraisal there should be no surprises. Supervision will play an important part in making sure that there are continual discussions about performance, competence and areas for development, and will therefore contribute to the quality of the appraisal process. As Morrison (2005) has identified, where performance management frameworks and HR processes are unclear or ineffective, the task of the supervisor in managing individual performance is made harder and in some cases impossible.

Managing performance through practice leadership

Throughout this book the social work supervisor has been positioned firmly in the role as a leader of practice, and the attributes of an outstanding leader are never more crucial than when they are working with others towards the best possible social work practice. For social work supervisors the stakes are high, as the expertise of their supervisees will have a profound effect on service users, who have a right to a competent service, as well as other stakeholders, including the organisation and partner agencies.

Chapter 1 explored some of the aspects of the leadership role within supervision, and this includes using every ounce of emotional intelligence to work sensitively yet firmly with performance issues. Research into what makes outstanding leaders (Tamkin *et al.* 2010) reveals that they manage to understand 'the importance of support, challenge, and providing a net, and if they do let someone fall they make sure it is with compassion and the lesson is learnt' (Tamkin *et al.* 2009, p.67).

Support and challenge need to be seen as part of the same process, yet too often supervisors may feel that by challenging their supervisees' practice they will be seen as less than supportive. Practice then reverts to the permissive supervision style, rather than achieving the authoritative style that is likely to result in the best performance (see Chapter 3).

There is the possibility that a permissive style is more likely where the organisation as a whole is perceived by the supervisor to be operating a blame culture. In this instance the supervisor may attempt to act as a buffer between the supervisee and the organisation. The result of this can be failure to challenge performance issues. Practice quality therefore declines, and the organisation as a whole becomes even more focused on individual blame.

Case study

Inspections had identified concerns about social work practice in a small unitary authority, and an external consultant was brought in to improve the quality of supervision. During sessions with front-line supervisors, it emerged that their main concern was the 'bullying' approach of senior managers, whom they described as presiding over a culture of blame that permeated the whole organisation. Graphic examples were given of senior managers threatening staff with disciplinary measures, restructuring teams with no consultation and interfering in day-to-day decision making. As discussions with the supervisors continued it also became clear that there were some areas where social work practice was clearly not good enough and that senior managers had a right to be concerned, although their way of dealing with this was extremely unhelpful. It also became clear that supervisors saw their role as protecting staff from senior managers and providing support. There was consequently limited challenge of practice, as supervisors did not want to be aligned with the culture of blame pervading the organisation.

Work with the supervisors focused on:

1. developing awareness of the dynamics that had been operating and their part in inhibiting performance improvements

2. giving supervisors frameworks for working positively with performance issues.

In addition, sessions were held with senior managers to feed back from the supervisors' sessions. Once senior managers were more confident that performance issues were being tackled, they were able to become less authoritarian in their approach, and the culture of the organisation began to shift towards learning and development rather than blame.

- Is this true for you?
- What strategies have you developed to address similar issues?

Practice leadership in this circumstance therefore needs to be supported by improvements in leadership throughout the organisation, as well as by giving supervisors tools and frameworks to increase their confidence in their own role.

What does managing performance through practice leadership actually involve?

How can supervisors lead practice in such a way that they support, challenge and keep an eye on the experience of service users at the same time?

In this role supervisors will have the responsibility to:

- attend to the conditions that are likely to support the best possible performance of supervisees

- openly recognise good practice and use this to enhance and develop performance (e.g. through the use of appreciative inquiry)

- make sure they have feedback from service users and other stakeholders about their experiences

- recognise and share early performance concerns and the meaning of related behaviour

- avoid using interventions that will set people up to fail

- use an understanding of individual motivation to promote change

- take formal action where change cannot be achieved (i.e. being clear about the bottom line).

These responsibilities are summarised in Figure 5.2, which provides a framework for the rest of this chapter.

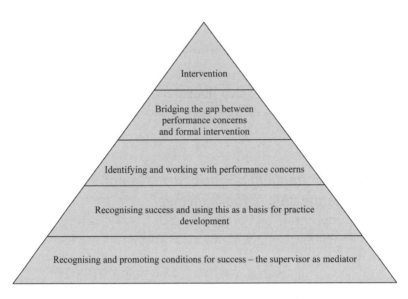

Figure 5.2 Managing performance through practice leadership

A point to consider

Reflecting on the triangle in Figure 5.2:

- Where do you currently direct most of your attention in working with individual performance? Do you feel this is the right balance?

Recognising and promoting conditions for success – the supervisor as mediator

Although this chapter focuses on the supervisor's work with the individual, it does not mean the task is only about working with that person. Enhancing the performance of the individual will only be possible if supervisors recognise their accountability for creating 'the conditions under which staff can successfully achieve their performance goals' (Latting and Beck 2004, p.204). It is in this role that the mediation function of supervision plays a crucial part.

Supervisors cannot, of course, be solely accountable for the conditions within which their supervisees work; however, the importance of their role as mediators lies in understanding the factors that might affect performance, recognising those that cannot be influenced by supervision alone, and working with the wider system to improve, wherever possible, the working environment. This may involve working with other supervisors and managers within the team to create a learning environment, providing feedback to the wider organisation about the impact of policies and procedures, and working to enhance relationships across the inter-professional network.

Awareness of their supervisees' work environment will therefore include the surface (and therefore more obvious) conditions, as well as those operating below the surface (such as team and inter-professional dynamics). Where there are problems in either of these domains the supervisory role must extend beyond the individual relationship to working with the wider system.

The idea of understanding 'below the surface' dynamics and their impact on the implementation of tasks and goals has been articulated by Huffington *et al.* (2004) in their exploration of the way in which unconscious factors affect organisational functioning. Armstrong (2004) argues that:

> Alertness to the emotional undertow of organisational life can be a powerful source of information for managers and leaders in enlarging understanding, reviewing performance, foreseeing challenges and opportunities and guiding decision and action. (Armstrong 2004, p.11)

For a more in-depth exploration of these ideas the reader will need to access the full text. However, for the purposes of this book it is important to recognise that one of the tasks of the supervisor in working with individual performance is to be sensitive to emotional undercurrents, find ways of exploring these with her supervisees and intervene in order to promote the context for successful practice.

In order to achieve this, one technique that the author has used is a form of mapping, to help understand what conditions are hindering practice and which are helping: Figure 5.3, for example, relevant factors are positioned so as to represent visually how far above or below the surface they are and the degree to which they help or hinder. It is most useful to have a discussion of this kind with all supervisees on a regular basis rather than waiting for a performance concern to arise.

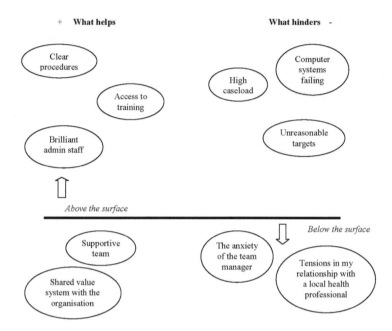

Figure 5.3 Factors affecting practice performance

Case study

Kerry was an experienced worker who had recently joined a team working with adults with learning disabilities. She was well known within the department as an excellent worker, yet her supervisor, the assistant team manager, was concerned because she did not seem very happy in her work and this had translated into poor/unmotivated/unfocused practice, with evidence of late recording and superficial assessments. Mapping identified that Kerry had found the team welcoming and friendly, the admin staff helpful and the team manager appreciative of her presence. She had quickly accumulated a high caseload and there had been a few computer glitches which had caused some difficulties with recording. However, although on the surface this was a friendly team, it was also a team under pressure with little time for members to support each other. The team manager assumed that Kerry could cope and wanted her to get on with the work without too much fuss. Further discussion revealed that the aspect of the work that Kerry found hardest was the approach of the team manager, which was very 'hands-on', and that she did not seem to trust in the capabilities of her staff. As she talked about this,

Kerry began to wonder whether in fact anxiety was at the root of the manager's behaviour, rather than lack of trust. Kerry also identified tensions in her relationship with a local psychiatrist who appeared to have unrealistic expectations about what the team could provide and caused her to feel 'battered' by constant requests to do more.

Having mapped the factors that are affecting practice performance, it is then possible to agree with the supervisee those that you can do something about directly, and those you will need to bring to the attention of others. For example, if the workload is beyond your control but it is genuinely affecting the capacity of the supervisee to practise effectively, this would need to be brought to the attention of others. It might, however, be possible to work on factors such as the relationship with a local health professional by facilitating a meeting, or by exploring the most effective way to manage this relationship.

In the case study above, mapping enabled the supervisor to consider what she might be able to do to develop a more productive context for Kerry. She decided to use her own supervision with the manager to allay any concerns she had about Kerry's competence, and to discuss the fact that they had unrealistic expectations of what Kerry could cope with by way of caseload. She also decided to arrange a three-way meeting with the psychiatrist to discuss the care plan and explore roles, responsibilities and expectations.

Improving individual performance through appreciative inquiry

Social work in England, particularly in the child care field, has, since the late 1980s, been influenced by a media focus on tragedies and poor practice, and this has led at times to a blame culture. This has meant that individuals at many levels of the organisation have been made to feel individually and personally responsible for practice failures, which seems in turn to have undermined confidence. The response nationally has been to develop more and more policies and procedures, which has further undermined and challenged the confidence of individual practitioners. Here, practice developments are about a desire to 'learn lessons' and 'stop mistakes happening again', rather than helping the workforce develop and grow. This, compounded by the new public sector management with its focus on managing performance via targets and compliance, has too often resulted in pressure on supervisors to 'manage performance' through a focus on tasks and outputs rather than the quality of practice. In this situation the developmental focus of supervision is driven by improving poor practice. Strengths-based approaches to social work supervision have too often been seen as a 'soft option' that fails to get to grips with poor practice and manage performance adequately. By failing to acknowledge and work with strengths, supervision can too often replicate the blame culture.

The positive expectations approach outlined by Morrison (2005) starts from the position that nobody gets out of bed in the morning with the intention of doing a bad job! In fact, the training courses run by the author nationally confirm the willingness and enthusiasm of staff at a number of levels to develop and learn. Most social workers will want to do their best, and it is the job of the supervisor to contribute to maximising the possibility they will be able to do so. A colleague has described this as akin to the 'washing-up syndrome'– a situation where the successful completion of a day-to-day activity such as washing up tends to be noticed and commented upon only when it isn't done, rather than when it is. As one supervisee commented, 'If I haven't done it there is a disparaging comment; if I have done it, it isn't even noticed.'

Appreciative inquiry (Cooperrider, Whitney and Stavros 2008) is a framework which, although developed with whole organisations in mind, has much to offer supervisors who are aiming to move beyond a deficit-focused approach to managing performance. The assumption underpinning this approach is that an organisation is a 'solution to be embraced':

> Appreciative Inquiry is the cooperative, co-evolutionary search for the best in people, their organisations, and the work around them... AI involves the art and practice of asking questions that strengthen a system's capacity to apprehend, anticipate and heighten positive potential. (Cooperrider et al. 2008, p.3)

Appreciative inquiry is based on the idea that organisations will 'grow in the direction they inquire'. If the focus is on identifying and solving problems, more problems will be discovered and there is a danger of a downward spiral of negativity which emphasises how to fail rather than how to succeed. If the focus is on what is working well, strengths can be built upon and used to feed into a virtuous cycle of continual improvement.

Appreciative inquiry questions focus on 'what is' (*discovery*) to help ignite the imagination about 'what might be' (*dream*) in order to co-construct a future in which the exceptional becomes everyday (*design*), and establish how to sustain this ideal (*destiny*).

Translating the principles of appreciative inquiry into the supervision environment, the focus is on using supervision to:

- ask questions about exceptional success

- explore and imagine what would happen if this became expected rather than exceptional practice

- consider how to move towards this goal and embed these ideas in practice.

Points to consider

1. Recall something that you did at work recently that went well, and you are really proud of the outcome.
   - What went well?
   - What happened?
   - How were you feeling at the time?
   - What did you do?
   - Did anyone else contribute towards the successful outcome?
   - What did they do?

2. What would happen if this type of success was a day-to-day occurrence?
   - How would you feel getting up and going to work in the morning?
   - Who else would be affected – what would they feel?

3. Is there one thing you could do that would help you move towards this being everyday practice?

- Who do you need to help you?

- What do you need to do?

4. How are you going to put this into practice?

Obtaining and receiving feedback

Social work frequently happens in the homes of children and their families, and often in private. This makes it difficult for supervisors to know about the quality of practice. How can they begin to identify where supervisees may need to work on developing and improving aspects of their practice? In fact, how often do we obtain direct feedback from service users and others who come into contact with our supervisees, in order to help with this task?

The idea of 360-degree feedback is now common in many management training programmes, but social work has struggled over the years to find ways of moving beyond a tokenistic approach to obtaining feedback from service users about the service they receive. Advances have been made, and it is now far more common for there to be service user representation on various groups and interview panels, as well as an increasing volume of research. What is less clear from talking to supervisors is how regularly they obtain feedback in relation to the day-to-day specific practice of their supervisees. Turner and Evans (2004) comment that:

> Practitioners are slow to develop ongoing processes to evaluate their work from users' perspectives. They need the opportunity to gain skills to collect users' views – ideally to work with users to identify priorities and give advice about the best ways of collecting users' views. (p.57)

Too often feedback to supervisors is in the form of a complaint rather than a compliment about good practice; consequently, ideas about performance may be skewed.

The role of observation

One way for supervisors to get a better understanding of the quality of their supervisees' practice is through direct observation. Once a social worker has qualified, it is possible that much of their work will be unobserved by others, and supervisors may be missing a rich source of information about their supervisees' direct interaction with service users. Taking opportunities to attend meetings with supervisees, and from time to time joining them on home visits, will allow for much richer conversations about practice approaches, interpersonal skills, strengths and areas for development. Where observation is not possible for any reason, a number of the tools referred to in Chapter 4 can help to give a picture of supervisees' day-to-day practice.

Supervisors need to ask themselves what they know about:

- the social worker's day-to-day practice with service users and other professionals

- how this supervisee's work is viewed by colleagues

- what a range of service users would say if asked about this social worker's practice.

Points to consider

If you know very little about how others view your supervisee's work:

1. Can your supervisee suggest ways of helping you to get a more rounded picture?

2. Are there already processes in place within your organisation/team for obtaining feedback from service users and other stakeholders? Can you utilise those?

3. Can you use supervision more effectively to gain a picture of supervisees' impact on others – could you ask different questions?

A WORD ABOUT PROVIDING FEEDBACK

Feedback will only be useful if it helps learning and practice development. Using the positive expectations framework outlined earlier in the chapter, feedback should be about continual learning and development, and identifying positives and strengths, as well as areas for improvement. It is equally important to consider how feedback is given, as this will either help or hinder this process.

Giving and receiving feedback is a skill that is utilised most successfully within an organisation where it is the norm, rather than an exception. If the culture of the team is one where giving feedback is a routine activity and everyone participates in conversations about practice, receiving feedback should not be a problem. However, if the culture is one where there is little interaction and sharing of ideas among team members, it is more likely that feedback will be perceived as negative and critical rather than part of a process of continual learning and development.

Think about the difference between team A and team B: in team A the atmosphere is quiet and everyone is focused on making sure they are completing the records on the ICT system. A social worker comes in from a visit and immediately switches on his computer and gets to work. This is a general pattern in team A, with case discussion confined to supervision and team meetings focusing on business.

In team B a social worker comes back from a visit and sits by a colleague to ask for a moment of time to run an idea past her. This becomes a whole-team conversation with everyone chipping in with ideas about what the social worker could have done differently and what to do next. After ten minutes' conversation the social worker returns to his desk and the room is quiet again. In this team there is always a slot in team meetings for case discussions and sharing of ideas about practice. It is not hard to see that workers in team B are more likely to be open to receiving feedback and able to use it constructively to improve their practice.

Recognising early performance concerns

As previously identified, working with performance concerns is challenging. However, one factor is key here – the longer concerns are left, the more complicated they are to deal with. Morrison (CWDC 2009b) entitled his chapter on managing performance 'Nipping it in the Bud', conveying a clear sense of the need to work effectively with early, low-level concerns in order to prevent escalation, which is unfair on supervisees and service users alike.

Supervisors should find that when using the supervision cycle outlined in Chapter 2, concerns about practice will automatically emerge, in contrast with the 'quick fix' approach where it is much easier for them to be hidden from view. Early concerns will emerge more readily when social workers are encouraged to describe their interactions with others, reflect on their own attitudes, values, feelings and biases, and use theory and research to inform their practice. Where the focus is on tasks achieved, quality of practice and the capacity of workers to feel and think, as well as do, will be far less clear.

It is important that there are regular, routine discussions within supervision about the factors that affect performance. Then, when performance concerns emerge, both supervisor and supervisee will have a head start in unpicking what is contributing to the performance issue. That does not mean that working with the issue will not be challenging. There may be feelings of discomfort for either party, and there is unlikely to be one simple explanation, but rather a combination of causal factors stemming from a range of sources. Trying to understand why concerns are emerging is fundamental to being able to manage them effectively.

Understanding why – a systemic approach

It is important to take a systemic approach to understanding what causes performance issues. Serious case reviews in children's and adults' services have recognised that it is necessary to move beyond 'blaming· individuals' for practice errors that lead to harm. These reviews also look at the context in which people work, the impact of organisational (and national) demands, and the quality of supervision, as well as individual responses to the demands of the work. In trying to understand 'why' performance concerns arise, it is important to consider the same key factors:

• the impact of the organisational context

• the quality of supervision provided

• the personal response to the demands of the role

• the skills and knowledge gaps.

A helpful framework for an initial analysis of early performance concerns is outlined below. It can be a way of identifying issues across the four key factors and can help individuals understand the multiple influences on day-to-day practice. It also provides an early, proactive approach to addressing the concerns in different parts of the system.

Table 5.1 Framework for initial analysis of early performance concerns

Factors	Action required
Organisational issues	
Quality of supervision	
Personal response to the demands of the role	
Skills and knowledge	

Case study

Darius was a newly qualified social worker who was having difficulties with getting his assessments completed. He was frequently coming to supervision with lots of ideas about a case but appeared unable to formulate these ideas within an assessment report. He was given the analysis of performance concerns framework to help him reflect on what was causing the difficulties before coming to supervision. The supervisor then worked with Darius on solutions, and added in her own perspectives. This then became a collaborative and problem-solving approach.

Table 5.2 Example of completed framework for analysis of early performance concerns

Factors	Action required
Organisational issues	
Work overload.	Agreement to explore Darius' workload – linked to time management.
Failure by the organisation to provide resources required – e.g. inefficient IT systems/ proper software and resources for dyslexic staff, etc.	Supervisor to make sure impact of any workload issues is relayed to senior managers. Raise the issue of dyslexic staff and their IT needs with senior managers, in line with disability legislation.
Quality of supervision	
Lack of clarity and explanation as to what was expected of him?	Session planned to focus on expectations of assessments.
Unrealistic deadlines set by the supervisor.	
Personal response to the demands of the role	
Poor time management.	Strategies to improve time management - possible diary exercise.
Personal stresses related to content of cases resonating with personal issues.	Review nature of caseload. Make Darius aware of staff counselling service. Make sure that there is an opportunity within supervision to reflect on anxiety generated by the work.
Dyslexia.	Bring strategies developed at university to manage his dyslexia to supervision for discussion.
Anxiety about making professional judgements.	
Skills and knowledge	
The supervisee's inexperience in writing this type of report?	Training sessions on report writing. Agreement to review first drafts.
The supervisee's poor report-writing skills	'Buddy' system to be set up with more experienced team member with expertise in report writing.

Root cause analysis

Root cause analysis is another method of considering factors affecting performance, which has been used widely in health settings in order to explore the cause of mistakes in practice (NHS 2004). The approach encourages consideration of a range of explanations for why errors might have been made, and introduces the idea of 'latent' organisational or systems failures that may contribute towards individual practice errors. The method has been refined and developed by the Social Care Institute for Excellence (www.scie.org.uk) in its approach to serious case reviews (Fish, Munro and Bairstow 2008).

Morrison (Morrison and Wonnacott 2009a) adapted these ideas using a diagram (see Figure 5.4) to illustrate how decisions and processes at the top of an organisation can generate problems that undermine clarity, communication, accountability, knowledge, skills and systems further down the organisation. He found that these become factors that can lead to both intentional mistakes and unintentional slips which breach organisational controls and defences such that a concerning incident occurs. (Morrison unpublished)

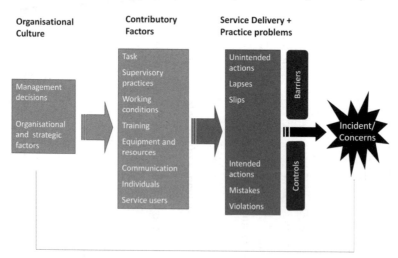

Figure 5.4 Latent Error Path

For example, an error such as not seeing a child on their own may be caused by a social worker lacking confidence in communicating with children because he is new to this aspect of social work. In this model, the supervision process itself may be part of the problem, with a supervisor giving the unspoken message that it is not OK to admit to gaps in knowledge. Lack of training provision by the organisation may also be an issue.

Understanding competence

The competence matrix (see Figure 5.5) developed by Morrison (2005) links well with the supervision cycle, and is another practice development tool. Used sensitively it can enable a focused discussion within supervision about the best way of moving forward together. Supervisors on training courses have reported sharing the matrix with their supervisees and discussing from each perspective where supervisees feel they are in relation to their practice in a particular case or practice context.

Warning: This should not be embarked upon where there are very serious performance problems. It is, however, useful as a tool in less emotionally charged situations, where it can help to identify different perceptions on the part of the supervisor and supervisee. By naming these, a constructive way forward is made more likely.

COMPETENCE MATRIX

Conscious competence	Conscious incompetence
What I know I can do	Areas of openly acknowledged gaps or weaknesses
Clear transferable skills	
Can be explained to others	
FIRM GROUND ZONE	**CHALLENGE ZONE**
Unconscious competence	Unconscious incompetence
What I know or can do without being conscious of how I know it	Things which I am unaware I don't know
Hard to explain to others and may be lost in conditions of stress	Others see gaps but I don't
	Root of performance problems
DEVELOPMENT ZONE	**DANGER ZONE**

It is important to remember that workers will move in and out of each of the segments depending upon external factors including the nature of particular pieces of work.

Figure 5.5 Competence matrix

Social workers who are in a 'firm ground' zone are likely to be able to move around the supervision cycle with relative ease. Social workers in the 'challenge' zone will openly recognise areas of weakness, and work with the supervisor to deal with these. Social workers within the 'danger' zone are likely to resist engaging with reflective supervision.

A particular challenge for supervisors is recognising and working with social workers who work intuitively and generally perform well (described as unconscious competence). For many workers this is a zone where the skills are so well developed that they do not need to think about what they are doing all of the time. This is similar to driving along a familiar road every day without consciously thinking about every detail of what you are doing and why you are doing it. This works well whilst there are no problems on the road, but as soon as there is an unexpected hazard the driver needs to be able to switch back into conscious competence. The problem arises if the driver's skills are not firmly based on understanding of what he is doing, and he is unable to adapt to changing circumstances. For social work supervisors it is crucial to understand whether the apparently intuitively competent worker is operating from a sound basis. The work of Munro (2008), which identifies the need to integrate both intuitive and analytic reasoning, points to the importance of using the reflective and analytical phases of the supervision cycle to develop an understanding of whether the social worker is working from a 'folk intuitive' or an 'expert intuitive' perspective.

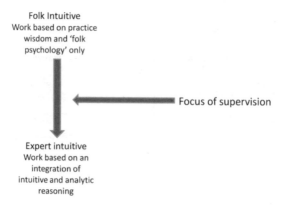

Unconscious competence

Folk Intuitive
Work based on practice
wisdom and 'folk
psychology' only

Focus of supervision

Expert intuitive
Work based on an
integration of
intuitive and analytic
reasoning

Figure 5.6 Unconscious competence

A supervisor may find, for example, that a social worker who has a reputation for expertise in engaging and working with families where there is a concern about neglect cannot explain why she is confident that the situation for children in the household is good enough. The focus of supervision may be in helping her to develop the knowledge and skill to be able to move beyond a solely intuitive approach and assessment to one which is firmly based on research evidence regarding the impact of neglect on child development.

By working together with supervisees to really understand the influences on their practice, the supervisor can be more precise about the origin of any early performance concerns and 'nip these in the bud' by developing strategies that work, rather than setting people up to fail.

Points to consider

Reflecting on the competence matrix:

- Where would you place yourself in your role as a supervisor?
- What does this tell you about your own development needs?

The set-up-to-fail syndrome

Research aimed at better understanding the relationship between the style of leadership and performance of employees (Manzoni and Barsoux 1999) identified that poor performance is often influenced by the unconscious behaviour of managers. Manzoni and Barsoux coined the phrase 'set-up-to-fail syndrome' to describe the dynamics of a relationship where the manager responded to concerns about performance by increasing the time, attention and instructions given to the member of staff. The research found that this behaviour, rather than improving performance, had the opposite effect. The employees reacted by perceiving a lack of confidence in their capabilities, and either withdrew from work and the manager's attention, or overreacted by rushing around chaotically trying to improve the supervisor's image of them. In either event, they failed to improve performance.

Case study

Tanya was concerned about the practice of one of her supervisees, Sam, who until recently had appeared to be a diligent worker, often praised by service users for his commitment. He had double-booked his diary on a couple of occasions and had missed the deadline on an important report. Sam was the only black worker in the team, which worked with a predominantly black and minority ethnic caseload, and Tanya was keen to keep him. She decided to invest more time in supervising Sam, meeting weekly to give him clear targets whilst at the same time making a number of training opportunities available to him. However, the result of this was that Sam felt under scrutiny and that no matter what he did, it would not be good enough. Colleagues, seeing how much supervision he got, believed that he was not up to the job and began to be critical of his practice. This demoralised him even more, and his practice began to deteriorate further as he avoided supervision and any discussions about his work.

It is not hard to understand the unintended consequences of Tanya's behaviour for practice. It is possible that Sam feels so disempowered by the supervisor that he increases authoritarian behaviour with service users in an attempt to regain some control. Behaviour in this circumstance might be risk-averse and pay minimal attention to understanding things from the service user's perspective. A second possibility is that withdrawal and lack of motivation led to Sam giving up, failing to challenge where required and developing a collusive relationship with service users. In this situation there might be an inappropriately high tolerance of risk.

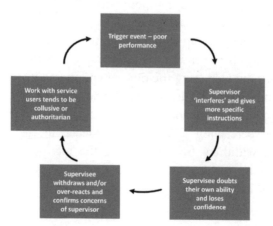

Figure 5.7 The 'set-up-to-fail' syndrome

Manzoni and Barsoux's research pointed to the need for managers to consider, first, that their own behaviour might be contributing to any performance problem. Using the findings from the research, the Social Care Institute for Excellence (SCIE; website link at the end of this chapter) suggests that at this point it is vital to prepare properly and use self-questioning to separate personal feelings from objective reality. Questions you may wish to ask yourself are:

- Were our interactions always so difficult?

- Has something changed in the relationship?

- Was the employee always this bad? In fact, is she really as bad as I believe?

- What hard evidence do I have to support this view? In precisely which areas is the employee weak?

- Could there be other factors, aside from performance, that led me to label this person a weaker performer?

- How did we reach this point?

- To what extent has my behaviour contributed?

Using the example above: Tanya's own behaviour was contributing to the problem, and this needed to be recognised before moving on. However, how far she was able to recognise this would depend upon the quality of her own supervision. If the supervisor did not feel able to discuss the issues with her own supervisor, the opportunity might be lost to explore how far the concerns were based on evidence about a general deterioration in Sam's practice, or were related to isolated incidents. In addition Tanya needed to explore whether her responses were a reaction to her own anxiety about losing Sam, rather than the best way of tackling the performance concern.

Having had an opportunity to reflect on what part the supervisor may be playing in the process, Manzoni and Barsoux's research suggests that a five-stage process should be used to break the cycle.

Tackling the 'set-up-to-fail' syndrome: five stages

1. *Create the right context for discussion.*
   This book is about social work supervision where there is a long tradition of using one-to-one meetings to explore

performance concerns. However, the *right context* is not always in place. Supervision that is not based on a relationship of honesty, trust and a clear agreement is unlikely to provide the environment where difficult issues can be explored.

2. *Agree the symptoms of the problem.*
   This involves arriving at a position where both supervisor and supervisee agree that there is an area of practice that needs improvement (e.g. a report is not up to the required standard). The time allowed for this phase should not be underestimated, with both parties needing to consider carefully their understanding of the practice improvement required.

3. *Arrive at a common understanding of what might be causing the weak performance.*
   At this point the root cause analysis approach, or Table 5.3 above, might be useful in exploring the possible contributory factors. Are these related to the supervisee and his relationship with the supervisor, or to latent organisational or system problems?

4. *Arrive at an agreement about performance and relationship objectives.*
   The supervisor and supervisee need to agree not only where they need to get to, but also how they are going to work together to get there. In other words, they need to set clear, achievable goals, backed up by the right support mechanisms – for example, agreeing what a good report will look like next time and what needs to happen to support the supervisee in making this happen. The supervisor may need to mediate with the organisation about supplying the most appropriate software for the dyslexic supervisee or reconsider case allocation in order to prevent overload.

5. *Agree future methods of communication*
   This stage involves the supervisor and supervisee reflecting on the conversation and agreeing preventative measures for the future. They may have acknowledged that the supervisee finds it hard to ask for help and that she will do so earlier rather than later in the future. Or the supervisor may undertake to ask the supervisee whether she needs any support as soon as a problem is noticed, rather than leaving it to become entrenched.

Table 5.3 Potential causes of weak performance

Organisational issues	Personal issues
• Work overload • Failure by the organisation to provide resources required – e.g. inefficient IT systems/ proper software and resources for dyslexic staff, etc.	• Poor time management • Personal stresses • Dyslexia
Inadequate supervision	**Skills and knowledge**
• Lack of clarity and explanation as to what was expected of them? • Unrealistic deadlines set by the supervisor	The supervisee's inexperience in writing this type of report? The supervisee's poor report-writing skills

Although, when set out in a logical sequence, avoiding the set-up-to-fail syndrome seems obvious, in practice it can be all too easy to notice a problem with performance and leap straight into setting performance objectives (i.e. telling the supervisee how the task should be done) rather than taking time to explore the interim steps. Manzoni and Barsoux note the emotional investment required to work on a day-to-day basis in a way that prevents setting people up to fail: openness of approach, availability to discuss problems as they emerge, and genuine willingness to challenge one's own assumptions and prejudices. All this points to the need for support for supervisors themselves, a topic which is explored in the last chapter of this book.

The 'set-up-to-fail' syndrome is a similar process to the 'short circuit' (see Chapter 2) where lack of reflection or analysis leads to interventions which move straight from the problem to the solution, with no understanding of why things occur. This lack of understanding 'why' always leads to inappropriate or unhelpful interventions – leaving social workers and families 'set up to fail'.

Setting people up to fail can happen at the organisational and team level as well as the individual level. The plethora of procedures and directives following the inquiry into the death of Victoria Climbié (Laming 2003) are now recognised as having unintended consequences (Munro 2010b), and there are examples of individual organisations mistakenly thinking that by focusing on instructing staff to meet targets and follow procedures, practice would automatically improve. This has not been found to be the case.

Understanding the meaning of behaviour

In the set-up-to-fail syndrome the behaviour of the supervisee performs a particular psychological function. By withdrawing from the 'interfering' supervisor the social worker aims to protect himself from further criticism by distancing himself. Other behaviours which are perceived as problematic may also be functional for the supervisee, and unless this is understood, strategies used by the supervisor to improve performance may backfire.

How can attachment theory help?

One way that supervisors can better understand the behaviour of their supervisees is by moving beyond a 'one size fits all' approach to managing performance concerns, particularly in relation to understanding responses to anxiety-provoking situations. Attachment theory helps to explain this, as it is a way of understanding the human response to anxiety.

Attachment theory has become extremely influential in social work practice with children and families (Howe 1995, 2005; Howe *et al.* 1999), particularly since advances in neuroscience have provided evidence of the significant relationship between brain development and the quality of relationships between infants and their primary caregivers, and this has brought fresh understanding of both need and risk. There has also been interest in how attachment theory might explain leadership behaviour (Fraser 2007), as well as the challenges facing supervisors managing poor performance (Morrison 2005).

Understanding attachment can provide supervisors with a model for explaining the responses of supervisees when faced with practice situations which raise their anxiety levels. There is no space here for a detailed explanation of attachment theory, and readers who are unfamiliar with the concept will find a comprehensive but succinct account in Howe (2010). In short, attachment behaviour is the behaviour that infants display at times of need and arousal in order to gain proximity to their caregivers. This includes crying, smiling, following and reaching out to the caregiver. Particular patterns of attachment (Ainsworth *et al.* 1978) will develop, depending upon the caregiver's response to the infant as the infant adapts to a particular style of caregiving. It is these adaptive responses that are likely to be triggered whenever the developing child is faced with situations that make her anxious.

In adulthood these established patterns may result in behaviours that range from mild to acute, depending upon the individual and the practice context within which he is working.

- *Secure attachment patterns* develop through consistent parenting where the caregiver is available and responsive to the child's needs. The child develops a sense of self-worth and, crucially, is more likely to have the capacity to reflect on and manage her own emotional state. Consequently, 'Individuals with these capacities have more behavioural options in situations of challenge. They cope better under stress' (Howe 2010, p.189).

- *Insecure avoidant attachment patterns* develop where carers find demands difficult to manage and respond to the child's need for proximity by distancing themselves from the child. Children respond by realising that their displays of attachment behaviour will usually result in reduced availability of their caregiver, and that the best way to gain a positive response is by downplaying the attachment behaviour. Under stress, this pattern in children and adults results in a tendency to avoid confronting emotions in themselves or others, a focus on compliance and keeping to the rules, and difficulty in asking for help. Difficulty in asking for help is particularly relevant in the supervisory relationship, and supervisors need to be aware of situations where the supervisee may not bring to the supervisor's attention issues that are causing him concern. Fraser (2007, p.46) notes that 'Equilibrium is maintained as long as things are under control and not too much is asked. If not there is anxiety or outbursts of anger. Impatience with others' attachment needs is frequent.'

- *Insecure anxious/ambivalent attachment patterns* develop where parenting is inconsistent and caregivers are not good at always recognising their child's attachment signals. Children in this circumstance adapt by making sure that their signals are heard, by increasing their attachment behaviour.

  When under stress, the emotions of adults with this pattern of behaviour will be on the surface, and they will be highly sensitive to the way in which others respond to their need for attention. They will find rational analysis hard and will be driven by their feelings, and the supervisor may find it hard to offer them sufficient support to satisfy their needs.

- *Insecure disorganised attachment patterns* typically develop from situations where the child has been abused or severely neglected by her primary caregiver. The person the child would wish to approach to help her reduce her anxiety is the one who is harming her, and she is therefore placed in an impossible situation. Finding strategies to manage this situation is virtually impossible and children are left in a situation of hyper-arousal, caught up in their own distress. Forming relationships in this situation is hard, trusting others is unlikely, and there may be a tendency to attempt to regain some control through controlling behaviours.

  This pattern results in adults who have no strategies for managing anxiety and are highly vulnerable when faced with a need to manage stress in the workplace. This vulnerability may exhibit itself in retreat (long-term sickness) or acting out distress through bullying and controlling others.

Warning: Focusing on understanding attachment patterns needs to be done in the context of all the other factors that will be contributing to performance at work. When working with performance issues, understanding attachment is just one part of the jigsaw and is not intended to pathologise individuals, but rather to help understand the meaning of behaviour in order that the supervisor can tailor an appropriate response. Fraser, discussing attachment patterns and leadership, notes:

> This is not a potential Belbin or Myers Briggs where the insecure can hide behind the nomenclature, but rather a very

personal way of looking at our tender histories, accepting their rich inheritance and understanding ourselves more fully and those we lead. (Fraser 2007, p.48)

Insecure avoidant and anxious attachment patterns are adaptive behaviours which many well-functioning individuals will be employing on a day-to-day basis. Both supervisors and supervisees bring their own patterns to the supervisory relationship, and the trick is to understand the strengths and challenges associated with the resulting dynamic.

Points to consider

1. Are you aware of the way you react under pressure? How does this relate to the patterns described above?

2. How would you describe the patterns of those you supervise? How does this affect how you work together?

3. What might be the impact of the following pairings on (a) the supervisory relationship and (b) outcomes for service users?

   • insecure avoidant supervisor and supervisee

   • insecure avoidant supervisor and insecure ambivalent supervisee

   • insecure ambivalent supervisor and secure supervisee.

Understanding 'stuck behaviour' – the blocked learning cycle

The blocked learning cycle (Morrison 2005), which uses the Kolb (1988) learning cycle as a visual framework, draws on attachment theory as the basis for understanding more fully why some supervisees behave in a way that triggers concerns about their performance. Morrison develops Crittenden and Claussen's (2000) outline of the functions of attachment behaviour to describe the supervisee's need to:

1. achieve safety under threat

2. elicit comfort when distressed

3. find proximity or closeness when alone

4. achieve predictability to regain control when the context is unpredictable or out of control

5. reframe job responsibility in a way that is tolerable.

(Morrison 2005, p.204)

Some concerns about performance may be understood in terms of the supervisee trying to fulfil these needs, and in so doing becoming blocked in his capacity to move around the supervision cycle.

As supervisees exhibit different patterns in the way they manage anxiety, they respond in various ways when faced with personal or professional challenges. Their response may inhibit their capacity to engage with all aspects of the Kolb (1988) learning cycle, and consequently may be seen by their supervisor as an intractable performance problem, rather than behaviour that can be understood and worked with. For example, the supervisee who responds to anxiety by seeking reassurance from others may find it hard to move on from the 'reflection stage', whereas the supervisee who tends to cope by keeping emotions under tight control may become stuck in 'analysis' where the predominant requirement is intellectualisation rather than emotional engagement.

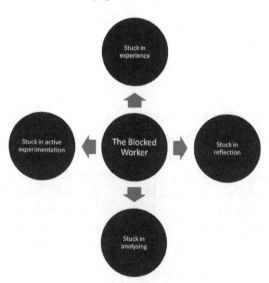

Figure 5.8 The blocked worker

The task of the supervisor is therefore to notice the behaviour and also to try to understand its function in relation to the management of anxiety, in order to work most effectively toward change. This draws not only on an understanding of attachment but also on a range of other factors, including the overall professional context and the experience of the social worker. For example, it will be important to understand the supervisee's supervision history, as the stuck behaviour could stem from a previously poor experience of supervision.

Working to achieve practice change

Having identified performance concerns and reached some level of understanding with the supervisee about the causal factors, the next task will be to work together to achieve practice improvements.

Giving feedback

We have already identified that feedback should be part of the day-to-day interaction within a social work team. If that is already the case, giving feedback about a particular performance problem will be far less difficult, and more likely to provide a sound basis for conversations about practice improvement. Any strategy aimed at performance improvement needs to include an element of direct feedback, which needs to be:

- planned – it is not helpful simply to react in the moment
- as close to the event as possible
- owned by the supervisor – not simply reporting the views of others
- specific, and focused on behaviours rather than personality
- focused on strengths as well as deficits.

(Adapted from Morrison 2005.)

Strategies linked to the blocked cycle

For a full exploration of strategies linked to the blocked cycle, the reader is encouraged to refer to Morrison (2005). Table 5.5 summarises some of the strategies that you may wish to consider.

Table 5.4 Understanding the functions of blocked behaviour

a: what may you notice?	Possible functions of the behaviour?
Reflection 1. Preoccupation with own feelings. 2. Inability to see the big picture. 3. Tasks not completed. 4. Dependency on the supervisor.	Self-protection to avoid having to deal with the anxiety induced by the work itself. Focus on own vulnerability reduces challenge by others. May result from being asked to undertake new or complex work and feeling overwhelmed, out of their depth and fearful of getting it wrong.
Analysis 1. Feelings suppressed. 2. Intellectualising. 3. Rigid adherence to procedures with little flexibility. 4. Challenging the supervisor's right to supervise.	Reduces anxiety through gaining a sense of control, safety and predictability. May be linked to resentment where the supervisor was previously a colleague and has been promoted; personal issues related to power and control; or a realisation that they do not feel comfortable with the emotional demand of the job.
Active experimentation 1. Actions dominate. 2. Unable to describe reasons underpinning actions. 3. Needs to be needed and creates dependency. 4. 'Maverick' behaviour.	Busyness reduces engagement with emotionally demanding or complex issues. 'Helpaholic' behaviour may be linked to their own emotional needs. This may result from previous lack of attention to emotional impact or be due to being hooked into the 'set-up-to-fail' syndrome.
Experience 1. Paralysed – unable to feel, think or do. 2. Cynical and negative. 3. Hyperanxious.	Withdrawal may be a means of coping with a toxic work setting or unresolved personal issues. This may result from: 1. a recent traumatic experience, such as threats from a service user which were not managed well, or a significant personal event. 2. burnout as a result of poor supervision over many years.

Practice change through motivation

There is a developing practice literature focusing on assessing and promoting service user motivation to change (Martino, Carroll and Ball 2007; Miller and Rollnick 2002; Morrison 2010a), but this is less frequently applied in discussion about supervision approaches. This is perhaps surprising because, if supervision is about developing individual practice, change must be an inherent part of the process. This should be what makes supervision exciting for both parties as they work together to negotiate complex systems, manage risks and find innovative ways to meet the needs of service users. Part of the process of supervision will be about encouraging changes in practice and it is essential that the motivation of staff, and their capacity to change, is accurately gauged and promoted.

The change cycle

One of the best known models that can help us to work towards change is the change cycle (Prochaska and DiClemente 1982). This is described clearly by Morrison in *The Child's World* (2010b) as follows:

> The change model describes five main elements of an intentional change process: contemplation, decision, action, maintenance and lapse. In addition the model describes two barriers to change; pre-contemplation and relapse. Although originally presented as a sequential 'stages' model in which individuals moved progressively through the five stages of change, the notion of 'stages' was later replaced by a more iterative or spiral idea. Change occurs more as a two steps forward and one back process. However, the experience of each change, even if unsuccessful, is such that we can never actually go back to square one, whatever it feels on a bad day. Hence although [the model] appears to present change as a linear process the reality is messier, the boundaries between different stages more diffuse and timescales unique to each individual. (p.312)

Table 5.5 Strategies linked to blocked behaviour

Stuck at –	Possible strategies
Reflection	• Understand what her worst fear is about the work. • Break tasks into manageable chunks. • Initially increase frequency of supervision in order to follow up on task completion. • Focus on strengths and what went well.
Analysis	• Do not avoid questions relating to feelings – stick with it. • Use your own supervision to consider whether issues relating to difference such as gender are a root cause. Check these out with the supervisee. • Use and value his analytical skills and knowledge base. • Do not get into an intellectual battle that you cannot win. • Keep a focus on how theory can help his practice. • Follow up on task completion.
Active experi-mentation	• Review her workload in order to understand whether the busyness is real (i.e. has the team fuelled the problem by giving her too much work?) • Ask her to keep a diary for a week in order to review time management. • Insist on supervision – do not allow it to be cancelled. • Focus on feelings about the job. • Slow the pace down by making sure at least one case is reviewed in depth each session. • Where there are underlying personal issues, consider how the organisation can provide the appropriate support. (Do not become their counsellor.)
Experience	• Carefully explore contributory factors. • Work with motivation – what attracted him to this job role and what needs to happen to regain initial enthusiasm? • Identify support needs. • Discuss training or retraining opportunities. • Keep an eye on the bottom line – i.e. capacity to provide a safe, effective service.

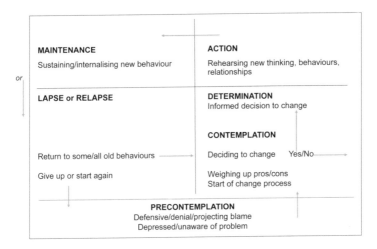

MAINTENANCE	ACTION
Sustaining/internalising new behaviour	Rehearsing new thinking, behaviours, relationships
LAPSE or RELAPSE	DETERMINATION
	Informed decision to change
	CONTEMPLATION
Return to some/all old behaviours	Deciding to change Yes/No
Give up or start again	Weighing up pros/cons
	Start of change process
	PRECONTEMPLATION
	Defensive/denial/projecting blame
	Depressed/unaware of problem

Figure 5.9 A comprehensive model of change

PRE-CONTEMPLATION

The danger is that the supervisor will see that practice change is needed and expect the supervisee to engage immediately with actions towards practice development – whereas in reality the supervisee may still be at the pre-contemplation stage. It is important to recognise this and give the supervisee time to reflect on any feedback that has been given about performance. There are obvious links here with avoiding the set-up-to-fail syndrome, where one of the first tasks has to be agreeing together that there is an aspect of work that needs to change. The change model provides an understanding of what needs to happen in order to move successfully from this point (problem identification) to strategies for working together to improve practice.

CONTEMPLATION

In avoiding the leap to inappropriate action, one stage in the process that is particularly crucial is that of contemplation. Morrison breaks this down into seven steps. Using the example of a social worker who is reluctant to take cases involving disabled children, the steps may look like this:

1. I accept that there is a problem (I lack confidence in working with disabled children).

2. I have some responsibility for the problem (I have avoided taking those cases).

3. I have some discomfort about the problem (I am worried that this stems from unconscious prejudices).

4. I believe that things must change (I want to develop this aspect of my work).

5. I can see that I can be part of the solution (I can take steps to develop skills in this area of work).

6. I can make a choice (I can actively build up this aspect of my caseload).

7. I can see the next steps towards change (I will go on the next 'communicating with disabled children' training course).

ACTION

The seven steps of contemplation should help the move to action, with the supervisee identifying for herself some of the steps she needs to take to move on. Dialogue is of course crucial, with the supervisor acknowledging his own part in the process and actions that he needs to carry out in support of the supervisee. Continuing the example above, they may both agree that training alone is not the answer, and that arranging time to work for a day with a paediatric occupational therapist would be a way forward.

This is where the supervisor may need a number of tools in his toolkit depending on the situation. For example, other techniques such as mentoring or coaching may be useful as an addition to the supervision process.

MAINTENANCE

The change model refers to internalising the new behaviour. The social worker taking her first assessment relating to a disabled child will need to explore in supervision how that went, what she felt about it and what she could have done differently. As she becomes more at ease with this aspect of her work, she will be able to move to a more intuitive understanding of what is needed, based on 'recognition of similarities with past experiences' (Fook *et al.* 1997). This is akin to the development of expertise and the development of a secure professional identity. Morrison states that as practitioners develop, and are helped to do so, they move to a more intuitive understanding, based on pattern recognition derived from a wide repertoire of experiences of similar situations. Ability to analyse and act becomes more contextualised and rapid – and in so doing a qualitatively different mode of practice emerges in which practitioners are able to reflect in action, draw from a variety of knowledge and skill bases, and develop strategies appropriate for the situation/context.

LAPSE AND RELAPSE

The other key feature of this model in relation to supervision is the expectation that people are unlikely to get it right on the first occasion. So that real change requires continual effort and follow-up. Built into supervision there needs to be an assumption that the supervisee may not get it right first time, there are likely to be challenges, and supervision is the place where these can be explored. Contingencies need to be in place and built into supervision, with the expectation that from time to time supervisees will struggle, however experienced they are. Munro (2008) suggests that 'The single most important factor in minimising errors is to admit you may be wrong' (p.125), with the clear message to supervisors that providing the space for discussion of both success and error is a vital part of any developmental process.

You may wish to consider a time when a supervisor helped you to improve your practice

1. What was your reaction when it was first suggested to you that you could do things differently – how did you feel?

2. Can you recognise moving through the seven steps of contemplation?

3. What encouraged you to continue trying if you relapsed at any point?

Working towards an optimal environment for practice change

Understanding this as a process is one thing; actually working with it in supervision when there are worries about someone's practice requires supervisors to draw on their interpersonal skills and provide an optimal environment for change to occur.

One model for helping with this has been developed by Michael Simmons ('Influencing without Executive Authority – Advanced Consulting Skills'. Copies available from Simmons@si-di.com). It uses the idea of commitment to change being most likely in an environment where there is a healthy dissonance about performance or behaviour with regards to both satisfaction and security, and each of these are at a medium level. If a social worker:

- is very insecure, it is unlikely that he will be very open to change regardless of his level of dissatisfaction, except in the special circumstances where things are so bad, he feels he has little to lose

- has a high level of security and medium or high dissatisfaction, she is very likely to be open to change, except that she is unlikely to feel that she needs outside help and this may present challenges for the supervisor

- feels very secure and has little or no dissatisfaction, he is unlikely to want change

- has a medium level of security and medium or high dissatisfaction, she is very likely to be open to change and will welcome the help of an external change agent such as a supervisor

- feels medium security and has little or no dissatisfaction, he is still unlikely to want to change.

Dissatisfaction and Security

Highly dissatisfied with the present situation	**?**	**Wants to change and will seek help**	Likely to change but unlikely to feel that they need any help
Some dissatisfaction	**Can't Change - STUCK**	**Willing to change, with help**	Willing to change but may not feel that they need any help
Little or no dissatisfaction	**Won't Change**	**Won't Change**	**Won't Change**
	Feels very insecure	Feels medium security	Feels very secure

in respect of the change they need to make

= how confident do I feel about being able to make the change?

Figure 5.10 Building commitment to change – dissatisfaction and security

The aim of the supervisor is to help the social worker reach the levels where change is possible.

The satisfaction continuum needs to be addressed first. This will require ensuring that the worker is satisfied enough with his practice to be able to engage with change in a constructive and measured way. This may well require focusing on the positives, whilst still being clear about what needs to be achieved, or reducing any sense of complacency.

If security levels are *low* and need to be increased, work will need to focus on role requirements and expectations and to provide the right support for these to be achieved. If security levels are too *high* combined with little or no dissatisfaction, there will need to be a reminder that the bottom line is the organisational consequences, through either disciplinary or capability procedures, but that the aim is to avoid this if possible. If high security levels are addressed before satisfaction levels, resistance is likely to increase and lead to polarised positions, reducing the chances of change occurring.

Managing and working with individual performance: the interface of supervision, mentoring and coaching

It is once we start to think about ways of developing staff through supervision that confusion sometimes arises between the respective functions of supervision, mentoring and coaching. In the experience of the author, social work organisations commissioning management training often ask for a confused mixture of supervision, mentoring and coaching, without any real clarity about what each involves. They are three distinct activities, but part of the confusion arises from the fact that they have similar skills at their heart and all have their place in developing individual performance. The supervisor may, for example, use coaching skills as part of the supervision process (CWDC 2009b), but supervision is not coaching, and one should not be substituted for the other.

Mentoring involves a relationship between a more experienced and a less experienced colleague, where the more experienced person helps the other to develop her knowledge and skills within the workplace. This is different from supervision in that the mentor is not accountable for the practice of his colleague, and the agenda is negotiated, but primarily led by the mentee. The focus of the relationship is on helping the mentee to develop her knowledge and skills.

Coaching definitions are many and varied, but fundamentally it is a process whereby the coach works with someone to define a skill gap and desired goals, and then supports him in finding solutions to get to where he wishes to be. The coach does not need to have expertise in the profession of her client – unlike the supervisor or mentor, who would be someone regarded as more expert in the relevant profession. Like mentoring, coaching skills may be useful to the supervisor and Morrison notes that: 'Where social work supervisors are using a coaching approach their knowledge is an essential contribution to this process both in identifying the need for improvement and in helping the worker to identify what "good" performance looks like' (CWDC 2009, p.97).

Coaching as one of the tools in the supervisor's toolkit may therefore involve using the skills and techniques of the coach to address a particular issue or performance concern, but coaching alone cannot take the place of a supervisory relationship. The relationship with the supervisor extends beyond a focus on developmental goals to concern with the emotional well-being of the supervisee and the impact this has on her capacity to make effective judgements. The bottom line for the supervisor is the responsibility to develop and maintain individual performance in order to meet most effectively the needs of the users of social work services.

Supervision and the 'bottom line'

Where supervisors, despite their best efforts, cannot feel confident that a social worker is practising safely, they will then need to engage with the formal processes within their organisation. There is also their responsibility to inform, where necessary, the relevant professional registration body. Some supervisors will feel supported in this task by their organisation, and others will feel less so. In all cases this is likely to be a point where considerable support is needed from their own supervisor – an aspect of supervision which is addressed in the next chapter.

Conclusion

One of the aspects of the supervisory role that marks the change from social worker to supervisor is the responsibility the supervisor has for understanding and managing the practice of another. This often presents challenges, and without the right supports and frameworks for understanding, supervisors may resort to extremes of behaviour and be perceived as either oppressive or uninterested in their supervisees' performance. The task (which is not always easy) is to balance the identification of areas for improvement with learning from good practice and interventions that do not set people up to fail. As with other areas explored in this book, the process here will work best where the organisational framework is clear, the foundations for supervision are strong, the relationship is sound and there is a high level of self-awareness on the part of both supervisor and supervisee.

Issues from this chapter to discuss with your supervisor

1. As a team, how do we identify good practice that everyone can learn from?

2. What frameworks do we use to understand early performance concerns?

3. What tools are there to develop practice competence? For example, is there the opportunity to supplement supervision with mentoring or coaching?

4. Am I clear about the HR procedures, processes that should be used where there are performance concerns that have not been amenable to change through early intervention? Where can I access support in this area of work?

Further reading and resources

Morrison, T. (2005) *Staff Supervision in Social Care.* Brighton: Pavilion. (Chapter 6 'The Blocked Cycle: Frameworks and Strategies'.)

SCIE *Managing Poor Performance.* Available from www.sciepeoplemanagement.org.uk/resource/docPreview.asp?

CHAPTER 6

Postscript

Supporting and Developing the Supervisor

Key messages from this chapter

- Good social work supervision will happen when supervisors are trained, supported, developed and supervised.

- The principles of good supervision apply to supervisors too.

- Developing supervisors needs to include training, mentoring and coaching underpinned by opportunities for action learning and supervisee feedback.

This chapter is entitled 'postscript', not because supporting and developing supervisors is an afterthought, but because all of the principles of good supervision explored in this book apply to supervisors too. Social work supervisors are one of the 'cornerstones' of the organisation, and on a day-to-day basis carry out a challenging role which can make a key difference to service users, social workers and their organisations. Despite this, too often supervisors on training courses have reported that they do not receive the type of supervision they are expected to deliver, and that they have been thrown into the role with little training and preparation. It is hardly surprising that front-line managers within the public sector, where most social work in England takes place, experience high levels of stress (Worrall, Cooper and Campbell 2001). The impact of this was recognised in the report by the Social Work Task Force (2009), which recommended that all organisations employing social workers should make a commitment to a strong supervision culture through:

- a clear supervision policy
- effective training and performance management for supervisors
- strong leadership and example from senior managers
- monitoring the actual frequency and quality of supervision against clear statements of what is expected
- compliance with established guidance on the features of good supervision.

What does this mean in practice?

1. All social work supervisors have the right to their own supervision. In England this right is enshrined in the General Social Care Council code of practice for employers. Employers should have policies for: 'Effectively managing and supervising staff to support effective practice and good conduct and supporting staff to address deficiencies in their performance' (2.2).

2. The supervision of supervisors should adhere to the organisation's overall standards for supervision and include opportunities for case discussion (where appropriate), support, reflection on the supervisor's own development and his role as a supervisor of social workers.

3. Where the manager of a supervisor is unable to provide all the elements of supervision, this may need to be supplemented by other activities, such as action learning and peer support.

4. Ways need to be found for supervisors to receive feedback from their supervisees on the impact of their supervision, and to use this to work together in partnership towards continual improvement.

Points to consider

On a scale of 1–10 (1 = low, 10 = high), how do you rate the quality of supervision and support you receive as a supervisor in the following areas?

1. I receive regular, formal one-to-one supervision.

2. I have a supervision agreement with my supervisor which is regularly reviewed.

3. Supervision focuses on my role as a supervisor and helps me to reflect on my supervision skills and relationships with my supervisees.

4. The supervision I receive includes emotional support and a focus on my own development as a supervisor.

5. I am encouraged in supervision to discuss feedback from my supervisees as a basis for improving my performance as a supervisor.

Where scores are 5 or below, what action can you take to improve the supervision you receive?

The supervisor's journey

Starting out

In Chapter 4 we explored understanding supervisees' perspective of assessments in relation to their role, their identity and view of self. This model also provides a framework for understanding the transition that supervisors make as they move from a social work to a supervisory role, and is particularly apt when moving between these roles within the same team.

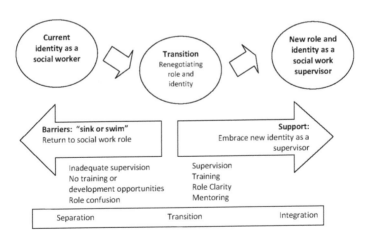

Figure 6.1 A new supervisor's journey

Based on a model developed by Morrison and used to describe the transition from student to newly qualified social worker (CWDC 2009a), Figure 6.1 represents the process that a new supervisor is likely to go through.

At the start of the journey, the degree to which the new supervisor successfully establishes her new identity is likely to depend upon:

- organisational factors, including a supervision policy that sets out the role and clearly mandates the supervisor to supervise

- the availability of training to increase confidence and role security

- supervision which allows for the exploration of uncertainty and anxiety and encourages skill development

- the availability of a more experienced supervisor as a mentor.

At this stage, mentoring is likely to be the most appropriate form of extra support, as the one-to-one relationship with a more experienced supervisor can provide the opportunity for the new supervisor to explore supervision challenges, drawing on the mentor's experience, skills, advice and expertise.

Consolidating and developing expertise as a supervisor

As the supervisor becomes established in his role, his development needs will tend to mirror those of the social worker he is supervising. In fact, all the issues that have been explored earlier in this book apply here as well – only more so.

Social work supervisors are dealing on a daily basis with complex decisions, and supporting their supervisees within an often turbulent organisational context. They are absorbing many anxieties from those in front-line practice, may be practitioners themselves, and have the added element of accountability for the standard of others' practice. The quality of their own supervision is therefore crucial, as is the opportunity for reflecting on and developing their own skills.

At this point feedback from supervisees can provide the basis for moving forward as a supervisor. The supervisee feedback questionnaire (adapted from Morrison 1993) is one way of obtaining feedback, reflecting on this with the supervisee and the supervisor, and identifying skill gaps and areas for development.

Table 6.1 Supervisee feedback questionnaire

Supervision	Usually	Some-times	Never
1. Is regular and uninterrupted.			
2. Is based on a negotiated agreement.			
3. Helps me to be clear about my role.			
4. Challenges my thinking.			
5. Helps me to reflect on my relationship with service users.			
6. Explores the use of power and authority in my work.			
7. Encourages consideration of working with diversity in my practice.			
8. Allows for the expression of anxiety.			
9. Explores the emotional impact of social work practice.			
10. Encourages the use of research to assist analysis.			
11. Helps me to explain the reasons for my judgements and decisions.			
12. Reflects my preferred learning style.			
13. Encourages learning from good practice.			
14. Identifies skill and knowledge gaps.			

Table 6.1 Supervisee feedback questionnaire *cont.*

Supervision	Usually	Some-times	Never
15. Encourages me to identify mistakes.			
16. Explores the reasons for poor performance.			
17. Identifies development opportunities.			
18. Is a medium through which my voice can be heard higher up the organisation.			
19. Makes a positive difference to my practice.			
20. Makes me enthusiastic about social work.			

Three areas I would like my supervision to improve are:

The things I could contribute to achieving this are:

(Adapted from Morrison 1993).

Once areas for development have been identified, coaching can provide a useful addition to supervision for supervisors as they gain experience in the role. There are various coaching models, many of which do not require the coach to have specific knowledge and skills relating to the role of the person being coached. These models are therefore most suitable for supervisors who are well grounded in the principles and practice of good supervision, offering an opportunity for supervisors to explore their own skills set and seek their own solutions, rather than for the novice supervisor, who will need to work with someone who can help her to identify what 'good' supervision looks like.

Action learning and supervisor development

Action learning sets are a source of supervisor development and support that can run like a thread throughout the development journey from new to experienced supervisor. They provide an excellent opportunity for supervisors to learn from each other, to feel that they are not alone in their situation, and to develop a shared language around the issues facing them. Morrison's (2010a) exploration of the strategic leadership of front-line practice notes that: 'Action Learning sets also play a key role within organisations in promoting shared standards, solving organisational problems and sustaining often poorly supported front line supervisors and managers' – and goes on to identify the contribution action learning sets can make by providing a structured space where supervisors can:

- feel safe enough to acknowledge their true feelings

- recognise uncertainty and doubt as a powerful aid

- get connected to and engaged with other supervisors

- tell it like it is (not how the organisation would like it to be)

- share knowledge, information and know-how

- contribute to the solution of each other's problems

- regain a sense of collective value and competence as supervisors

- recharge their batteries and refocus their energies.

(p.325)

Action learning sets are based on the following principles:

- Learning involves actually taking action, not just talking about it.

- Action involves work on a project/problem that is significant for the supervisor.

- Learning is a social process.

- The social process is carried out through group meetings.

- Groups are helped to learn by exposure to problems and each other.

- There is a facilitator.

(Mumford 1995, quoted in CWDC 2009a)

The process (Figure 6.2) can be an empowering one for supervisors, and at their best action learning sets create a culture of appreciative inquiry where supervisors' anxieties can be acknowledged, and where they can be reconnected with the possibilities of their role, challenged, and motivated to move forward, in an environment where they know they have understanding and support from their peers and that matters have become a shared organisational responsibility.

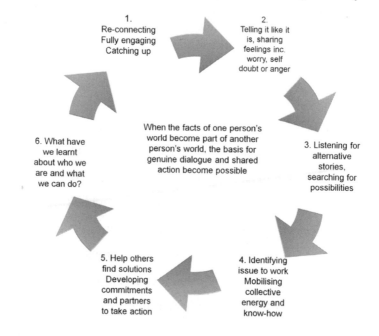

Figure 6.2 The process of action learning

Finally – what do all supervisors need?

All supervisors need to develop a level of awareness of their own needs as a supervisor, and to:

- engage in a dialogue with the organisation about the culture and systems that can support and sustain supervisors in developing effective supervision

- take responsibility for discussing their needs with their own supervisor

- reflect on what they can do as an individual to develop internal and external supports that will sustain them in the role.

Use Figure 6.3 to reflect on what is needed to sustain and develop you in your supervisor role.

1. What is in place already and what is missing?

2. What can you do differently?

3. What can you ask others to do differently?

4. How will you know when things have improved?

Figure 6.3 What do supervisors need?

REFERENCES

Ainsworth, M.D.S., Blehar, M., Aters, E. and Wall, S. (1978) *Patterns of Attachment: A Psychological Study of the Strange Situation.* Hillsdale, NJ: Lawrence Erlbaum.

Armstrong, D. (2004) 'Emotions in organisations: disturbance or intelligence?' In C. Huffington, D. Armstron, W. Halton, L. Hoyle and J. Podey (eds) *Working Below the Surface: The Emotional Life of Contemporary Organisations.* London: Karnac Books.

Baumrind, D. (1978) 'Parental disciplinary patterns and social competence in children.' *Youth and Society 9,* 239–276.

Bell, L. (2009) *Child Welfare Professionals' Experience of Supervision. A Study of the Supervision Experiences of Professionals who Attended 2009 Congress.* York: Baspcan. Available at www.baspcan.org.uk

Berne, E. (1964) *Games People Play: The Psychology of Human Relationships.* London: Penguin.

Brandon, M., Belderson, P., Warren, C., Gardner, R., Howe, D., Dodsworth, J. and Black, J. (2008a) 'The preoccupation with thresholds on cases of child death or serious injury through abuse and neglect.' *Child Abuse Review 17,* 313–330.

Brandon, M., Belderson, P., Warren, C., Howe, D., Gardner, R., Dodsworth, J. and Black, J. (2008b) *Analysing Child Deaths and Serious Injury through Abuse and Neglect: What Can We Learn?* Research report DCSF–RR023. London: DCSF.

Brown, A. and Bourne, I. (1996) *The Social Work Supervisor.* Buckingham: Open University Press.

Bunker, D. and Wijnberg, M. (1998) *Supervision and Performance: Managing Professional Work in Human Service Organisations* San Francisco, CA: Jossey Bass.

Skills for Care/CWDC (2007) *Providing Effective Supervision.* Available at www.skillsforcare.org.uk

Cherniss, C. and Goleman, D. (2001) *The Emotionally Intelligent Workplace.* San Francisco, CA: Jossey-Bass.

Children's Workforce Development Council (2009a) *NQSW Guide for Supervisors.* Available at cwdcouncil.org.uk

Childrens Workforce Development Council (2009b) *Guide for Supervisors: Early Professional Development.* Available at www.cwdcouncil.org.uk.

Children's Workforce Development Council (2010) *Newly Qualified Social Worker Programme: Evaluation of the first year 2008-09.* Leeds: CWDC.

Cooperrider, D.L., Whitney, D. and Stavros, J.M. (2008) *Appreciative Inquiry Handbook.* Ohio: Crown Custom Publishing.

Cousins, C. (2010) '"Treat me don't beat me." Exploring supervisory games and their effect on poor performance management.' *Practice: Social Work in Action 22,* 5, 281–292.

Crittenden, P. and Claussen, A. (2000) *Organisation of Attachment Relationships.* Cambridge: Cambridge University Press.

Dalzell, R. and Sawyer, E. (2007) *Putting Analysis into Assessment.* London: National Children's Bureau.

Davies, R. (1998) *Stress in Social Work.* London: Jessica Kingsley Publishers.

Department for Education (2010) *Building a Safe and Confident Future: One Year On. Detailed Proposals from the Social Work Reform Board.* London: Department for Education.

Fauth, R., Jelicic, H., Hart, D., Burton, S. and Shemmings, D. (2010) *Effective Practice to Protect Children Living in 'Highly Resistant' Families.* London: C4EO.

Ferguson, H. (2005) 'Working with violence, the emotions and the psycho–social dynamics of child protection: Reflections on the Victoria Climbié case.' *Social Work Education 24,* 7, 781–795.

Fish, S., Munro, E. and Bairstow, S. (2008) *Report 19: Learning Together to Safeguard Children: Developing a Multi–Agency Systems Approach for Case Reviews.* London: SCIE. Available at www.scie.org.uk/publications/reports/report19.asp

Fook, J., Ryan, M., and Hawkins, L. (1997) 'Towards and theory of social work expertise' *British Journal of Social Work 27,* 399–417.

Fook, J., White, S. and Gardner, F. (2006) 'Critical reflection: a review of contemporary literature and understanding.' In S. White, J. Fook and F. Gardner (eds) *Critical Reflection in Health and Social Care.* Maidenhead: Open University Press.

Forrester, D., McCambridge, J., Waissbein, C. and Rollnick, S. (2008) 'How do child and family social workers talk to parents about child welfare concerns? *Child Abuse Review 17,* 23–35.

Fraser, D. (2007) 'Give me the child and I'll give you the leader. What can attachment theory teach us about leadership?' *International Journal of Leadership in Public Services 3,* 3, 42–48.

Gadsby Waters, J. (1992) *The Supervision of Child Protection Work.* Aldershot: Avebury.

Gardner, R. (2008) *Developing an Effective Response to Neglect and Emotional Harm to Children.* London: NSPCC.

Gast, L. and Patmore, A. (2012) *Mastering Approaches to Diversity in Social Work.* London: Jessica Kingsley Publishers.

Gibbs, J. (2001) 'Maintaining front line workers in child protection: a case for re–focusing supervision.' *Child Abuse Review 10,* 323–335.

Gibbs, J., Dwyer, J. and Vivekananda, K. (2009) *Leading Practice. A Resource Guide for Child Protection Frontline and Middle Managers.* Victorian Government Department of Human Services. Available at www.dhs.vic.gov.au

Goleman, D. (1996) *Emotional Intelligence: Why it Can Matter More than IQ.* London: Bloomsbury.

Haringey Local Safeguarding Children Board (March 2009) *Serious Case Review 'Child A'.* Available at www.haringeylscb.org. Published by Department for Education on 26 October 2010.

Harkness, D. (1995) 'The art of helping in supervised practice: Skills, relationships and outcomes.' *The Clinical Supervisor 13,* 1, 63–76.

Harkness, D. and Hensley, H. (1991) 'Changing the focus of social work supervision: Effects on client satisfaction and generalised contentment.' *Journal of Social Work 36,* 6, 506–512.

Hawkins, P. and Shohet, R. (1989) *Supervision in the Helping Professions.* Buckingham: Open University Press.

Heimann, P. (1950) 'On counter-transference' *International Journal of Psycho-Analysis 31,* 81–84.

Holland, S. (2004) *Child and Family Assessment in Social Work Practice.* London: Sage.

Holtz Deal, K. 'Effective Interpersonal and Critical Thinking Skills' In Austin, M.J. and Hopkins, K.M.(Eds) *Supervision and Collaboration in the Human Services* California, CA: Sage.

Honey, P. and Mumford, A. (2000) *Learning Styles Questionnaire (LSQ)*. Available at www.peterhoney.com

Howe, D. (1995) *Attachment Theory for Social Work Practice*. Basingstoke: Macmillan.

Howe, D. (2005) *Child Abuse and Neglect: Attachment, Development and Intervention*. Basingstoke: Palgrave Macmillan.

Howe, D. (2008) *The Emotionally Intelligent Social Worker*. Basingstoke: Palgrave Macmillan.

Howe, D. (2010) 'Attachment: Implications for Assessing Children's Needs and Parenting Capacity.' In J. Horwath (ed.) *The Child's World*. London: Jessica Kingsley Publishers.

Howe, D., Brandon, M., Hinings, D. and Schofield, G. (1999) *Attachment Theory, Child Maltreatment and Family Support: A Practice and Assessment Model*. Basingstoke: Macmillan.

Huffington, C., Armstrong, D., Halton, W., Hoyle, L. and Pooley, J. (2004) *Working Below the Surface: The Emotional Life of Contemporary Organisations*. London: Karnac Books.

Hughes, L. and Pengelly, P. (1997) *Staff Supervision in a Turbulent World*. London: Jessica Kingsley Publishers.

Janis, I. (1982) *Groupthink: Psychological Studies of Policy Decisions and Fiascos*. Boston, MA: Houghton Mifflin.

Kadushin, A. (1968) 'Games people play in supervision.' *Social Work 13*, 23–32.

Kadushin, A. (1976) *Supervision in Social Work*. New York: Columbia University Press.

Kiernan, K. and Mensah, F. (2008) *Poverty, Maternal Depression, Family Status and Children's Cognitive and Emotional Development in Early Childhood: A Longitudinal Study*. London: Centre for Longitudinal Studies.

King, P.M. and Kitchener, K.S. (1994) *Developing Reflective Judgement: Understanding and Promoting Intellectual Growth and Critical Thinking in Adolescents and Adults*. San Francisco, CA: Jossey Bass.

Kolb, D. (1988) 'The Process of Experiential Learning.' In D. Kolb (ed.) *Experience as the Source of Learning and Development*. London: Prentice Hall.

Laming, W.H. (2003) *The Victoria Climbié Inquiry: Report of an Inquiry by Lord Laming*. London: The Stationery Office.

Laming, W.H. (2009) *The Protection of Children in England: A Progress Report*. London: The Stationery Office.

Latting, J.K. and Beck, M. (2004) 'Facilitating Learning through Assessing Performance Goals.' In M.J. Austin and K.M. Hopkins (eds) *Supervision as Collaboration in the Human Services: Building a Learning Culture*. Thousand Oaks, CA: Sage.

Lexmond, J. and Reeves, R. (2009) *Building Character*. London: Demos.

Lexmond, J., Bazalgette, L. and Margo, J. (2010) *The Home Front*. London: Demos.

Littlechild, B. (2002) *The Management of Conflict and Service User Violence against Staff in Child Protection Work*. University of Hertfordshire Centre for Community Research.

McCracken, D.G. (1988) *The Long Interview*. Beverley Hills, CA: Sage.

Manzoni, J.F. and Barsoux, J.L. (1999) 'The Set-up-to-fail Syndrome.' In *Harvard Business Review on Managing People*. Harvard Business School Press.

Martino, S., Carroll, K., and Ball, S. *et al.* (2007) 'Teaching, Monitoring and Evaluating Motivational Interviewing Practice.' In G. Tober and D. Raistrick (eds) *Motivational Dialogue: Preparing Addiction Professionals to Motivational Interviewing Practice*. London: Routledge.

Menzies, I.E.P. (1960) *A Case Study in the Functioning of Social Systems as a Defence against Anxiety: A Report on a Study of the Nursing Service of a General Hospital.* London: The Tavistock Institute.

Miller, W.E. and Rollnick, S. (2002) *Motivational Interviewing: Preparing People for Change.* Second edition. London: Guilford Press.

Morrison, T. (1993) *Staff Supervision in Social Care.* Harlow: Longman.

Morrison, T. (2005) *Staff Supervision in Social Care* (revised edition). Brighton: Pavilion.

Morrison, T. (2007) 'Emotional intelligence, emotion and social work: Context, characteristics, complications and contribution.' *British Journal of Social Work 37*, 2, 245–263.

Morrison, T. and Wonnacott, J. (2009) Training materials

Morrison, T. (2010a) 'The Strategic Leadership of Complex Practice.' *Child Abuse Review 19*, 312–329.

Morrison, T. (2010b) 'Assessing Parental Motivation for Change.' In J. Horwath (ed.) *The Child's World.* Second edition. London: Jessica Kingsley Publishers.

Moscovici, S. and Zavallone, M. (1969) Quoted in Munro (2002) *Effective Child Protection.* First edition. London: Sage.

Mumford, A. (1995) 'Learning in action.' *Industrial and Commercial Training 27*, 8, 36–40.

Munro, E. (2008) *Effective Child Protection.* First edition. London: Sage.

Munro, E. (2008) *Effective Child Protection.* Second edition. London: Sage.

Munro, E. (2010a) 'Learning to reduce risk in child protection.' *British Journal of Social Work 40*, 1135–1151.

Munro, E. (2010b) *The Munro Review, Part One: A Systems Analysis.* London: Department for Education.

Munro, E. (2011a) *The Munro Review of Child Protection Interim Report: The Child's Journey.* London: Department for Education.

Munro, E. (2011b) *The Munro Review of Child Protection: Final Report: A Child–Centred System.* London, Department for Education.

NHS (2004) National Reporting and Learning Service. National Patient Safety Agency Root Cause Analysis Toolkit. Available at www.nrls.npsa.nhs.uk/resources/?entryid45=59901

Pottage, D. and Evans, M. (1992) *Workbased Stress: Prescription is Not the Cure.* London: National Institute for Social Work.

Prince, J., Gear, A., Jones, C. and Read, M. (2005) 'The child protection conference: A study of process and an evaluation of the potential for on-line group support.' *Child Abuse Review 14*, 113–131.

Pring, J. (2011) *Longcare Survivors: The Biography of a Care Scandal.* London: Disability News Service.

Prochaska, J. and DiClemente, C. (1982) 'Trans-theoretical therapy: Toward a more integrative model of change.' *Psychotherapy: Theory Research and Practice 19*, 3, 276–288.

Reder, P. and Duncan S. (1993) *Beyond Blame: Child Abuse Tragedies Revisited.* London: Routledge.

Reder, P. and Duncan, S. (1999) *Lost Innocents: A Follow-up Study of Fatal Child Abuse.* London: Routledge.

Reder, P. and Duncan, S. (2003) 'Understanding communication in child protection networks.' *Child Abuse Review 12*, 82–100.

Richards, M., Payne, C. and Sheppherd, A. (1990) *Staff Supervision in Child Protection Work.* London: National Institute of Social Work.

Ruch, G. (2000) 'Self and social work: Towards an integrated model of learning.' *Journal of Social Work Practice 14*, 2, 99–112.

Ruch, G. (2010) 'The Contemporary Context of Relationship-based Practice.' In G. Ruch, D. Turney and A. Ward. (eds) *Relationship-based Social Work.* London: Jessica Kingsley Publishers.

Rushton, A., and Nathan, J. (1996) 'The supervision of child protection work. *British Journal of Social Work 26*, 357–374.

Social Care Institute for Excellence (2009) Guide 27: *Leading Practice – a Development Programme for First-line Managers.* Available at www.scie.org.uk/publications/guides/guide27/index.asp

Schön, D. (1983) *The Reflective Practitioner: How Professionals Think in Action.* Aldershot: Arena.

Schön, D. (1994) 'Organisational Learning: The Core issues.' In *Organisational Learning.* London: Office for Public Management.

Simmons, M. 'Influencing without Executive Authority – Advanced Consulting Skills'. Available at Simmons@si-di.com

The Social Work Reform Board (2010) *Building a Safe, Confident Future –One Year On.* London: Department for Education.

The Social Work Task Force (2009) *Building a Safe, Confident Future. The final report of the Social Work Task Force.* London: Department for Education. Available at www.theworkfoundation.com/research/leadershipres.aspx

Stanley, J. and Goddard, C. (2002) *In the Firing Line: Violence and Power in Child Protection Work.* Chichester: Wiley.

Tamkin, P., Pearson, G., Hirsh, W. and Constable, S. (2010) *Exceeding Expectation: The Principles of Outstanding Leadership.* London: The Work Foundation.

Titterton, M. (2005) *Risk and Risk Taking in Health and Social Welfare.* London: Jessica Kingsley Publishers.

Tsui, M.S. (1997) 'Empirical research on social work supervision: The state of the art (1970–1995).' *Journal of Social Service Research 23*, 2, 39–54.

Tsui, M. (2005) *Social Work Supervision: Contexts and Concepts.* London: Sage.

Turner, M. and Evans, C. (2004) 'Users Influencing the Management of Practice.' *Managing Front Line Practice in Social Care.* London: Jessica Kingsley Publishers.

Wiffin, J. (2010) *Family Perspectives on Safeguarding and on Relationships with Children's Services.* London: Office of the Children's Commissioner. Available at www.childrenscommissioner.gov.uk

Wilson, K., Ruch, G., Lymbery, M. and Cooper, A. (2008) *Social Work: An Introduction to Contemporary Practice.* Harlow: Pearson.

Worrall, L., Cooper, C. and Campbell, F. (2001) ' The Pathology of Organisational Change: A Study of UK Managers' Experiences.' In B. Hamblin. J. Keep and K. Ask (eds) *Organisational Change and Development.* Harlow: Financial Times/Prentice Hall.

Wonnacott, J. (2004) The Impact of Supervision on Child Protection Practice: A Study of Process and Outcome. Unpublished M.Phil. thesis. University of Sussex.

SUBJECT INDEX

AUTHOR INDEX